# The Final Truth

Books by Ramesh S. Balsekar

*Your Head In The Tiger's Mouth*
*Consciousness Speaks*
Ripples (a booklet)
*The Final Truth*
*A Duet of One*
*From Consciousness to Consciousness*
*Experiencing The Teaching*
*A Net of Jewels*
*Consciousness Writes*
*The Bhagavad Gita* (commentary)
*Explorations Into The Eternal*
*Experience of Immortality*
*Pointers From Nisargadatta Maharaj*

# The Final Truth

*A Guide To*
*Ultimate Understanding*

by
Ramesh S. Balsekar

Advaita Press

Copyright © 1989 by

Ramesh S. Balsekar

First Published in United States Of America by

ADVAITA PRESS

P.O. Box 3479

Redondo Beach, California 90277

Edited and Designed by: Wayne Liquorman

Cover Design: John McClung

Printed by: McNaughton & Gunn

Library of Congress Catalog Card Number: 89-84930

ISBN 0-929448-09-X          0 9 8 7 6 5 4 3

# Table of Contents

# Preface

At the end of what had been intended as a two-weeks' stay, which got extended to almost four months of frequent talks, a Western visitor asked me a direct question: "What is the simple, final Truth?" And it suddenly struck me then that some question like that from a disciple must have been instrumental in creating the *Mahavakya*[1].

And yet the fact of the matter is that Truth cannot be described or explained. Truth is "What-Is" and the acceptance of it. Every word that is uttered concerning Truth can only be a pointer towards it. The understanding of Truth cannot be achieved. It can only happen. And it can happen only when the mind is empty of all thought, of all conceptualization. When it comes, it will almost certainly come suddenly, without any irritation, when it's least expected. And when it comes, it cannot be accepted unless the mind is empty of the "me" and the heart is full of Love.

The understanding, which is itself Truth, happens only when there is immediate and direct (and therefore "true") perception. It happens only in the absence of reason and logic, which are in duality. In such understanding the comprehender (the "me" as an individual entity) is totally absent and the mind is in total surrender. Understanding, as such, can only spring out of absolute silence, the stillness that prevails when action ceases and conflict ends.

What is the basis of this understanding? It is that all objects, all phenomena that are perceivable in the manifestation, are merely appearances in Consciousness. They are perceived and cognized by Consciousness itself through the "mechanism" of dichotomy into subject and object,

---

1. Upanishadic declarations expressing the highest Vedantic truth: *Prajnanam Brahman* (Consciousness is Brahman), *Aham Brahmasmi (I am Brahman), Tat Twam Asi* (That Thou Art) and Ayam Atma Brahma (the Self is Brahman).

supplemented by comparison between interdependent contraries. This is in effect the process of conceptualization.

Such understanding leads to the direct apperceiving of the nature of the human being. It is then clear that the phenomenal manifestation that is described as *maya* (the basic illusion) is not that of the process of life as birth-life-death, but a belief in the objective entity that goes through and experiences these conceptual occurrences. There is a supplementary illusion without which this basic illusion could not have been possible: space-time in which the illusory entity is extended. The "who", the "what", the "where" and the "when" are all conceptual images in Consciousness. They are all "real" as any mirage or dream.

This statement may need some explanation. The objects in the phenomenal manifestation (including the sentient beings), which are appearances in Consciousness, are not to be perceived as being "made" of mind-stuff, for they are just not there. They do not exist except as illusions, and therefore they cannot be "composed" of anything. The totality of manifestation, and everything therein, is Consciousness itself, the Unicity. All there is, is Consciousness, not aware of itself in its noumenal subjectivity, but perceived by itself as phenomenal manifestation in its objective expression. If this is understood in depth there is nothing more to be understood. Why? Because such understanding must comport the realization that there is no individual entity as such. What we *think* we are is merely an appearance, an insubstantial shadow, whereas what we really and truly *are*, is Consciousness itself, the formless Brahman. Understanding is the absolute and total annihilation of the identity which has been built up over the years. The final hurdle preventing the dawn of truth or apperception or enlightenment or awakening or whatever other word that may be used is *identification as a separate entity*. In other words, the individual may intellectually understand the illusory character of the entire universe and everything therein, *but not that of "himself"*! And that is the true power of *maya*: thinking, perceiving, living from the viewpoint of the illusory phenomenal center.

The final truth, as Ramana Maharshi and Nisargadatta Maharaj and all the sages before them have clearly stated, is that there is neither creation nor destruction, neither birth nor death, neither destiny nor free will, neither any path nor any achievement.

This is what this book is all about. So, if you have understood this, please accept my salutations — there can be nothing in this book for you. Truth is unchangeable, experienced from moment to moment — here and now — and never in duality. What this book does is to point to the final Truth from various angles, various directions and various aspects. The final Truth is Unicity.

Before closing, I must make a reference to the fact that the reader will certainly notice that certain points — even the very words — have been repeated at several places. This was necessary in order to give a sense of fullness and wholeness to the relevant matter. My request to the reader is not to pass through these repetitions cursorily and quickly as being mere "repetitions" but to consider them as being important for the reason that it was necessary to repeat them in the context of that particular aspect of the Truth which, in any case, can only be *One*.

RAMESH BALSEKAR
Bombay — March 1988

# BOOK ONE

*The Nature of the Phenomenal Manifestation*

# The Manifest World — Its Nature.

The basic difficulty about providing an example or illustration to explain a metaphysical principle is that while the metaphysical subject-matter relates to the Absolute, any illustration can only be at the relative level.

It is because of this difficulty that tradition usually takes three analogies *together* in order to enable the student to understand the apparent unreality of the manifested universe:

    (a) the rope mistaken for the snake;

    (b) the desert or wasteland on which the mirage appears as a startlingly real phenomenon; and

    (c) the personal dream with which is compared the waking state as the "real" dream state.

A rope is first mistaken for a snake; but when it is subsequently recognized as a rope, the rope is no longer a snake — the snake has ceased to appear. In this analogy, the argument that the universe is only an appearance, an objective expression of the real Self, does not seem to have adequate force, because, even after this information, the universe continues to appear as before, instead of ceasing to appear. The point here is that the snake can be manifestly shown to be a mistaken notion: the rope appears as a snake only in darkness and as soon as there is light, the mistake is clearly discovered. But the dissolution of the world-appearance can take place only through subjective, actual experience of the Self. In order to explain this discrepancy, use has to be made of the analogy of the mirage. Like a snake, the mirage is also a false appearance and can be objectively explained and proved; and the fact that the mirage continues to be seen even after it is known to be a false phenomenon proves that *the continued appearance of a thing is not proof of its reality.*

At this stage, a third difficulty arises in the form of this argument: The mirage is a false appearance because there is no water to quench the thirst; but the world, while it continues to appear, serves many purposes. This difficulty is adequately met by the analogy of the personal dream, in which food is eaten in the dream and satisfies the dreamed hunger of the dreamed character.

The analogy of the personal dream also meets another argument. While the mistaken notion of the snake and the illusion of the mirage can promptly be explained and understood, it is very difficult to explain away the fact that the world is something that contains rivers and mountains and other objects that are thousands of years old. We look around and see people busy with the business of birth and death and life as it is generally known. The personal dream meets this argument head on, because *the dream world contains all the relevant features of the actual world*: In dreams there are people living their lives, and rivers and mountains which have apparently existed a long time, although the dream may last only a few moments.

What the dream analogy demonstrates is the fact that desire and satisfaction — which seem to be the basic facts of life — are as unreal as the individual to whom the need and its satisfaction relate. As the Chinese Sage Chuang Tzu put it, "Is it Chuang Tzu who dreamt last night that he was a butterfly or is it the butterfly who is still dreaming that it is Chuang Tzu?"

In fact, there has been neither creation nor destruction. Bondage lasts only as long as mind invests a perceived object with reality. Once that notion disappears, with it goes the supposed bondage. Here, in this objectified creation, only that which is thus objectified grows and decays. It is in this conceptualization and objectification that the duality is conceived as the very basis of the manifestation. Duality is necessary so that manifested objects may be perceived and cognized in a frame-work of space and time in which the objects are extended. It is essential to bear in mind that while the manifestation thus created is of the nature of mere appearance or illusion, it is real enough in the sense that the manifestation is a reflection of Consciousness. The shadow has no substance or nature of its own, but without the substance the shadow cannot arise.

# The Arising Of I Am

Noumenon — pure subjectivity — is not aware of its existence. Such awareness of its existence comes about only with the arising of consciousness — I Am. In other words, Consciousness-at-rest is not aware of its existence until there is *a natural but sudden movement within itself*. It becomes aware of itself as I Am. This sudden movement is known by various terms such as *Omkar* (the primeval sound) in Vedantic literature, and perhaps as the big bang of astronomy!.

The spontaneous arising of I Am (as a movement in Consciousness) is the sense of existence, the sense of presence. It brings about simultaneously and concurrently the appearance in Consciousness of the phenomenal manifestation. The phenomenal manifestation necessitates *certain presupposed phenomenal conditions* without which such manifestation would not be possible. The wholeness and equanimity of the subjective noumenon (Consciousness-at-rest) gets apparently split into the duality of a pseudo-subject and an observed object. Each phenomenal sentient object then assumes subjectivity as a "me" in reference to all other objects as "others". The objectifications of this duality necessitates the apparent creation of the twin concepts of "space" and "time". Space is necessary for the volume of objects to be extended. Time (duration) is necessary for the phenomenal images extended in space to be perceived, cognized and measured in terms of the duration of existence of each object and event.

Human beings, like all other sentient beings (objects which can feel and sense their existence and presence), are as much an integral part of the total phenomenal manifestation as any other phenomena, such as rocks, streams and trees. They arise with the arising of the phenomenal universe precisely as they do in a dream, spontaneously and concurrently. *As objective phenomena there is no apparent difference between animate and inanimate objects*, but, subjectively, it is sentience which is responsible for enabling the sentient beings to *perceive* the phenomenal manifestation.

Sentience is an aspect of Consciousness (the primeval totality of energy), but it has nothing to do with the apparent *arising* of the manifestation within Consciousness. Although sentience enables human beings to perceive other objects (and intellect, another aspect of Consciousness, enables them to discriminate), human beings are not different as *phenomenal objects* from all the other phenomena.

The very essence of the ultimate understanding is that there cannot be any difference between the unmanifest noumenality and the manifest phenomenality. *Noumenality and phenomenality are identical* in the sense that noumenality is immanent in phenomenality. Phenomenality has no nature of its own other than noumenality. The shadow cannot have any nature of its own other than that of its substance. In other words, *phenomenality is the objective expression of the noumenal subject.*

It is the identification of noumenality with each separate phenomenon, producing a pseudo-subject out of what is merely the operational element in the human phenomenal object, that produces the phantom of an autonomous individual. This is the ego which considers itself to be in conceptual bondage. The *phenomenal functioning is quite impersonal. The illusory individual entity is wholly unnecessary therein, except as a mere apparatus or mechanism.* The impersonal functioning comports impersonal *experiencing* of both pain and pleasure. It is only when this impersonal experiencing is *interpreted* by the pseudo-subject as the experiencer experiencing the experience in duration that the experiencing loses its intemporal, impersonal element of functioning and assumes the duality of objectification as subject/object.

We use the expressions "various things" or "everything" or "all things", but they are just figures of speech. All that exists is universal Consciousness. The universe *as such* is not the universal Consciousness, but Consciousness *is* the universe, just as the bracelet is made of gold but the gold is not made of the bracelet. Whether the manifested universe exists or not, Consciousness is there as the subjective Absolute.

Just as the sculpted image is latent in the marble slab, so is the notion of "me" and "the world" latent in the potential plenum — the fullness — of the Consciousness when at rest. When the totality of the actual known manifests out of the totality of the potential unknown, it is known as creation. There is no deliberate action involved in this process of creation — the infinite Consciousness and the "creation" have no divided or separate relation between them.

Consciousness is immanent in all things, sentient and insentient. Though the rock and the tree may appear to be inert, there exists a relationship between them. The fundamental constituents are the same in both but combined in one way to form a tree and in another way to form a rock. Similarly, it is because of the similarity in the constitution of the fundamentals that the taste buds in the tongue respond to the "taste" in the food. Thus, *self-knowledge is actually a realization of the existing unity*, which has been incorrectly regarded as a relationship. The mistake results from the assumption by the split-mind of a dualism between subject/object and a host of other interrelated opposites.

There is no causal relationship between Consciousness and the universe. The truth is that Consciousness alone exists and is immanent in what appears as the universe. In other words, Consciousness and the universe are not two in which any sort of relationship could exist. It is perfectly correct to say that the tree exists in the seed because both have apparently separate forms. But in that which is formless, the Consciousness, how can it be said that the cosmic form of the universe exists in a seed-state? *There is no seed in the Consciousness which gives up its seedness in order to become the universe.*

Millions of universes appear in the infinite Consciousness (the *Chit-akasha*), forming a totality of the known form (the *Mahad-akasha*) in the totality of the formless unknown. These millions of universes appear in the infinite Consciousness like specks of dust, illuminated by a beam of light. Each individual universe merely reflects the the illumination, it is certainly not the cause.

The part played by Consciousness in the activities of the world is somewhat like the part played by the spring season in the flowering of the trees. "Sitting quietly, doing nothing, spring comes and the grass grows by itself". The experiencing through the multitude of psychosomatic mechanisms is actually done by Consciousness. Indeed it *is* Consciousness. The entire functioning in the manifested universe is Consciousness. It manifests somewhere as space, somewhere as time, somewhere as action, just as there is a variety of oceans and seas but really only one individual mass of water.

The infinite Consciousness is "like a creeper, with the sentient and insentient beings as its parts, sprinkled with the latent tendencies of countless beings, and endowed with past creations as filaments and desires as its buds".

No thought could arise or be expressed or be put into action except by the infinite Consciousness. Consciousness appears as the physical bodies (which are in fact inert) that experience various reactions through contact with one another in *its* aspect as sentience.

Consciousness alone is the reality, not only in all phenomenal objects, but also in all experiences. *It is from thought that action begins.* And thought is the function of the mind, which is nothing but Consciousness that has limited itself by identification with an individual psychosomatic mechanism.

Although reality is the one infinite, indivisible, homogeneous Consciousness, there appears, inexplicably, an apparent division or separation of the observer, that which is observed, and the function of observing. For observation to take place, there must be the apparent observer and the manifestation that is observed. In other words, the function of observing (or any other function of hearing, smelling, etc.) can only take place in apparent duality. But the significant point is that that which is the subjective I (Consciousness, the universal Self) is precisely what appears as the objective universe. There is no distinction between the two, just as there cannot be any distinction between air and its movement. *There is no causal relationship between the infinite Consciousness and the phenomenal universe.* In infinite Consciousness this universe appears like a particle of dust in the air.

The appearance of the universe in the infinite Consciousness cannot be rationalized as in the case of the relationship between waves and the ocean. While there is an apparent reality in the words "ocean" and "waves", there is no "thingness" which could be correspondent to the words "universe" and "mind" or "ego". The simple situation is *that the appearance of the universe exists in infinite Consciousness, just as the notion of distance or emptiness exists in space.* Whenever questions are raised and discussed about something like a mirage, it can only be on the basis that the mirage does not exist. The appearance of the universe and the mind (or the ego) has no existence in the absence of Consciousness. It is the cosmic energy of the Consciousness that has created the *illusion* of the world and the ego-sense out of a combination of the five elements (like the mirage is an illusion of water created by the rays of the sun on the heated sands). It is Consciousness alone that exists. It creates the illusion of the world-appearance and the ego-sense, and perceives the illusion of diversity in what is truly pure Unicity.

In the case of gold and golden ornaments, it can be seen that the ornament has been created out of the gold as an apparently separate thing, made at a certain time, at a certain place. *From the Consciousness, however, nothing separate has been "created".* As Consciousness rests in itself, and is all there is, there can only be subjective experiencing. There is neither matter nor cause for the "creation" of the universe. The universe is a mere appearance and the ego-sense is a mere concept. If this basic difference is not kept in mind, any similar illustration (which is necessarily in relativity) will cause considerable confusion.

The infinite, formless Consciousness exhibits in its objective expression its various aspects — intention, will-to-do or desire, space-time and natural order or *niyati* or destiny, and an infinite range of potencies or energies like knowledge, dynamics, and either positive or negative action. Although these aspects and potencies are notionally different in their manifestation and functioning, they are not different *in their essence* from infinite Consciousness (the primal energy).

The entire manifested creation presents a cosmic dance by the divine dancer, and *the dance cannot be differentiated from the dancer*. The dance is executed to the tune of time or duration, and takes place on the stage of space. The various movements are the various aspects and potencies. It is the potency of the natural order of events and sequences which presents the theme of the dance based on the specific characteristics of each object (from a blade of grass to the conceptual creator Brahma), reacting to the various events and sequences . The natural order (the *niyati*) is the dancer presenting the dance drama of phenomenal manifestation and its functioning. It is Consciousness which has spontaneously, causelessly, been stirred out of its state of rest into one of movement, by the cosmic thought "I Am". The dance exhibits various epochs and seasons and portrays moods of every conceivable nature, like love and hate, compassion and anger, etc. It is set against the background music of the elements, on a stage illuminated by the sun and the moon and the stars, with the *dramatis personae* provided by all the sentient beings in the entire universe.

The infinite Consciousness, though not different from its aspect as the dancer (natural order) and the dance itself, is the silent but alert witness — *drashta* — of this cosmic dance drama happening *within* itself.

It seems difficult to comprehend how the universe could exist in the infinite Consciousness that is supposed to be transcendental. Truly there is nothing other than Consciousness, and therefore Consciousness cannot but be immanent in everything that appears to exist. And yet no phenomenal manifestation can have any kind of relationship with Consciousness because a relationship can exist only between two different entities.

It is in this sense that Consciousness is transcendental to the manifested universe. The universe exists in Consciousness like future waves in a calm sea — only *apparently* different in potentiality. A crystal held over a colored object assumes the color of the object, but the color is not of any independent nature. Consciousness is not affected by the appearance of the universe within itself — it is transcendental — just as space is not affected by the clouds that float in it, or the ocean is not affected by the waves that arise on its surface.

The formless Consciousness can be experienced only through the multitude of sentient bodies with names and forms, just as light can be seen only through refracting agents. It is thus not that the multitude of names and forms exist independently of Consciousness but that Consciousness can express itself only through these forms. It is not the fans and the lights and the kitchen gadgets that work by themselves but it is the electricity that operates through these various forms.

What makes the seed sprout into its natural growth is Consciousness and nothing else. The first thought "I Am" within the Consciousness creates the apparent diversity in manifestation. As space, Consciousness enables the seed to exist; as air, Consciousness breathes 'life' into it; as water, Consciousness nourishes it; while as earth, Consciousness provides the base for the seed to sprout As light, Consciousness reveals its manifested form; while as sentience, Consciousness provides the means to perceive and cognize the manifested form. *Consciousness is all there is, expressing itself in various ways to bring about the manifestation and its functioning in totality* .

Consciousness, the supreme Brahman, both transcendental and immanent, infinite and intemporal, permeates everything. It enables human beings to experience sound, sight, taste, fragrance and touch. It is pure non-duality in essence. It is only ignorance that brings about the dualism of interrelated opposites, the most basic of which is subject/object, "me"/"not-me". And ignorance itself is a concept.

The sculptor "creates" different images from one rock. It may contain the figures of divine beings, their consorts, and their followers, but it continues to be a rock, carved or uncarved, in one block or as various figures. Similarly, the infinite cosmic Consciousness may be considered as one all-encompassing, homogenous mass of potentiality out of which are actualized millions of phenomenal objects of immense variety. The all-encompassing Consciousness always remains as Consciousness, with the phenomenal manifestation or without it. When the phenomenal objects are referred to by various names, the distinction is purely notional. The seed cannot contain anything other than itself, and whatever emanates from the seed, like flowers and fruits, can be nothing other than of the nature of that seed itself. The homogeneous mass of the Consciousness cannot give out anything other than what it is in essence. Consciousness *is* immanent in every phenomenal object in the manifestation that emerges in Consciousness.

When the truth is realized, and apperceived, all notions of dualism cease. Whatever is seen, in any form, can only be Consciousness because all is Consciousness, and all manifestation now or at any time cannot but be Consciousness. This is the final Truth.

Time, space and duality itself — adjuncts necessary for manifestation to occur — are all aspects of Consciousness, together with sentience. They are all notions or concepts or thoughts. With this realization dawns the further realization that while they are unreal *in themselves*, as aspects of Consciousness, they cannot be anything but Consciousness itself. There is basic unity in the potential diversity. We can speak of diversity in the phenomenal manifestation, as we speak of the water in a mirage. Just as all that is named as water is nothing but hydrogen and oxygen gases, similarly, all phenomenal manifestation is nothing but Consciousness, appearing as the mind, mountains, oceans, rivers, animals and human beings.

As the many-splendored feathers and wings of the peacock are potentially present in the egg of the peacock, so is the apparent diversity of the phenomenal manifestation potentially present in Consciousness. The manifested universe is therefore simultaneously dual and non-dual. Time, space, mind, ego, etc. have acquired illusory reality although they have not been created at all. Nothing has been created as a separate thing, though it may appear so.

Such expressions as "mind", "ego", "individual", "ignorance", etc. are used only as aids for those who seek their self-nature in the earliest stages. They are nothing but mere notions, without any inherent substance. The word "water" is used in the case of a mirage merely so that it can be understood that what *appears* as water is not water at all but an illusion. Similarly, various notions are used to show that what *appears* as diversity is not so and that what *appears* as reality is also not so! All is Consciousness.

In the apparent creation, Consciousness is in constant movement and has been ever since the thought I Am arose spontaneously (without any cause). This movement in Consciousness is the primal energy which is the reality in everything that apparently happens as inexorable causality in time. It is known by various names — *chit-shakti* (the primal energy), *mahashakti* (the great power), *mahadrishti* (the great vision), *mahakriya* (the great doing), *mahaspanda* (the great vibration), etc. It is the power which endows everything with its *dharma* (characteristic quality). It must, however, be firmly kept in mind at all times that this distinction between the Absolute and its power, Brahman and *shakti*, is purely notional. It is used merely to explain the manifested creation as the work of the power, which itself is only a concept. The distinction is as conceptual as the distinction between the body and its parts, or the body and the various functions therein, like the digestive system and the respiratory system.

The functioning of this *shakti* (power), known as *niyati* (destiny), determines all that happens, i.e., the arising of dispassion that leads to self-enquiry, the meeting between the *guru* and the disciple, and the fructifying or otherwise of the *guru's* teaching. The whole process is one of evolution in which the individuals are really quite irrelevant except as the instruments through which the process of evolution takes place and through which the *niyati* functions.

In a dream, the dream-bodies and everything else appear very real. The sensorial perceptions are as acute as in the waking state. But this reality disappears as soon as we are awake. When there is an awakening to our true nature, the reality of our bodies and the sensorial perceptions in what we call the waking state are seen to be as unreal as the dream-bodies. Deep sleep follows the end of the dream, so also when the seeds of thought and conceptualization are burnt into barrenness by pure knowledge, there is "liberation" from the waking dream. The liberated sage appears to think and live like any other person, but such living is like the shape which a rope might retain even after it is totally burnt. Liberation or true awakening, unlike the conditions of deep sleep or unconsciousness which retain the seeds of thought in a latent form, carries no remnants. The awakened live firmly established in the apperception that the universe, though a reflection of the noumenal absolute, is still merely an appearance. Their thoughts concern that and only that which is their real nature. Their speech and conversation, too, concern only that. Their perceiving of the phenomena and events is of the nature of witnessing without comparing and judging. Thoughts may arise spontaneously but they are not pursued, merely witnessed.

"I" am the subjective Reality, the dreamer of myself in the Cosmic dream in which I appear. I cannot therefore possibly be the objective, dreamed appearance and, therefore, too, I am not an entity. It is never the object that awakens, only the dreamer who awakens from the identification with the dreamed object that is the cause of the illusion of bondage. "Awakening" in effect, means vanishing as a dreamed object, the dissolving of appearance, the evaporation of the illusion or dream. Awakening therefore amounts to the discovery that the apparent entity has disappeared along with the total illusion or dream. The dreamed object is, in fact and substance, nothing other than the subjective Reality, now uncovered by the disappearance of the illusion.

Consciousness alone exists. When Consciousness is viewed through ignorance or unwisdom, what is experienced is the phenomenal universe, which is the physical aspect of Consciousness. When the infinite Consciousness (Brahman) mistakes itself in the phenomenal functioning for something other than what it really is, there arises self-experience, or "Self-destruction". At that point Consciousness limits itself to the mind, the very nature of which (as the content of mind) is to veil or to destroy Self-knowledge. Such veiling or destruction of the Self is only momentary or for a *kshana*. But in the mind that *kshana* is stretched into a world-cycle. Why? Because such is the nature of the mind — to create a notional or conceptual existence. Obviously, being only notional, such existence is unreal and ceases the moment the Truth is realized. The moment the proverbial rope is seen as a rope, the illusion or notion of it as being a snake disappears. As soon as Truth is realized, "self-destruction" is transformed into Immortality.

The delusion and confusion of seeing the phenomenal universe not as an illusion, but as real, is itself the mind. Non-comprehension of the Truth is itself the mind. Apprehension of the Truth means destruction of the mind (by exposing the mind as the fraud it is). This is what is called Self-knowledge or Self-realization or awakening or enlightenment. In other words, the clear apprehension, that "this" is kinetic consciousness (the mind) and not "That" (pure Consciousness), brings about the destruction of the illusion of the mind, precisely like the realization that "this is not water" brings about the destruction of the illusion of the mirage.

The destruction of the illusion of the mind simultaneously brings about the destruction of the allied illusion of the separation created by the "me" concept. All that exists then is the pure Consciousness. Thereafter, all living becomes noumenal in the sense that all ideas of what is to be done and what is not to be done become irrelevant and are abandoned as bubbles on the surface of the ocean of infinite Consciousness. The mind, relieved of all its conditioning, becomes totally unconditioned as *Satva,* or pure Consciousness, and does not see Consciousness as the phenomenal universe. All movement and non-movement in the infinite Consciousness is realized as merely notional, totally unreal.

It is Consciousness that activates the mind, just as it is the breeze that causes the rustling of the leaves. Consciousness makes the senses function "like the rider guides the horse". (An individual refers to Consciousness as "my Consciousness"!!) It is ironic that Consciousness, which is the lord of all physical bodies, should act like a slave, forever engaged in all activities throughout the universe!

The Truth should be realizable by anyone, but it is not, only because not everyone engages himself in self-enquiry. When "That" is seen, everything has been seen; when "That" is heard, everything has been heard; when "That" is touched, everything has been touched. The world is only because "That" is. "That" is awake even when we are asleep; "That" goads the ignorant dreamer into wakefulness; "That" removes the distress of the suffering, the bondage of the ignorant.

Consciousness is the void of space. It is the movement in all things moving. It is the light in all things luminous, the solidity in earth, the fluidity in liquids, the heat in fire. It is the cosmic energy in all things manifested. Whatever the body may be subjected to, Consciousness is not affected. How can there be any relation between Consciousness that we truly are and the desires and cravings of the body that we think we are?

Consciousness is the fragrance in the flower. Just as a forest conflagration, though itself a single body of flame, assumes many forms, so does the formless, non-dual Consciousness assume various forms as objects in the universe. Consciousness is the subtle solution of continuity in the innumerable universes which are forever potentially present in it, precisely as the flavor of the foodstuffs is potentially present in the ingredients but is made manifest by cooking them. All universes would instantly collapse like a house of cards if Consciousness were not. All concepts of pleasure and misery collapse in the presence of Consciousness, precisely like darkness collapses in the presence of light.

There is no awakening, no cessation of awakening; no birth, nor death. There is only pure Consciousness, in the presence of which the smallest and the subtlest appears micro-cosmic. Persons seen in a dream have no past *karma* — similarly, those that arose in the beginning of "creation" did not have any *karma*, as they were pure Consciousness. It is only when there is a firm rooting in the apparent reality of this phenomenal manifestation — and belief in the reality of volition of the individual — that the notion of *karma* arises. The individual in his apparent volition thrashes about in his "real" world and suffers because of his supposed *karma*. If it is realized that Brahman or Consciousness alone exists, and thus there is no creation as such, then where is *karma*? Whose *karma*? If the total creation is a non-creation, can the individual exist as an entity?

The totality of creation is in the heart of the infinite Consciousness, just as one's personal dream is in one's mind, both as the cause and the effect. I-am-ness is itself conceptual "creation". The interdependent opposites like virtue and sin, good and evil, positive and negative, subject and object, which create the separation that is the source of all suffering, are mere notions without any basis of reality. They have no independent existence. It is only the one pure infinite Consciousness which appears as diverse objects in a dream. These dream-objects disappear in deep sleep, precisely as this apparently real dream-world, which appears in our apparent waking-state, disappears in the cosmic dissolution which is the equivalent of the deep sleep state.

When this Truth is realized, how can there by any bondage or liberation?

There is nothing stable about the appearance of the world. It keeps on changing all the time, because change is the essence of manifestation (*anitya*), like the ever changing patterns of cloud-formations in the sky. It is not generally realized that there are innumerable worlds. It is ignorance which gives the feeling that this world is a stable entity. The fact of the matter is that each man's "world" is different from that of someone else, because each man's thoughts are not, can not, be fully known to anyone else. People living in the same house have different dreams in which are experienced different worlds.

Mind has the unique faculty of holding on to something as a notion. Such a notion is known traditionally as *samskara*. However, with the realization that a notion, a *samskara*, cannot have any independent existence other than as a mere movement in Consciousness, it loses all its force and influence. It is then realized that the *samskara* is only an intrinsic part of the ignorance, which itself is an illusion! All there is, is Consciousness.

"*Samskara*" is generally interpreted as "latent impressions of past actions and experiences", but here the word is used essentially to mean "something which existed before the arising of the dream" (and shines as something seen before). The *samskaras* created in the waking state arise in the dream, but they are also created anew in the waking state. The truth is that they were created in *what appeared to be the waking state*, but actually was not. Notions arise in Consciousness as naturally as movements arise in air — there is no need for *samskara* to create notions. What cosmic creation is, is the state wherein the experience of "ten thousand things" arises in Consciousness. The cessation of this experience is the cosmic dissolution. It is thus, that the pure infinite Consciousness (*Chit-akasha*) brings into being the diversity of names and forms without ever losing its unicity, precisely as one creates a world in one's dream. The "creation" is nothing but a mirror-reflection in the indivisible Consciousness and is therefore not different from the Consciousness itself. The cause (naturally existing before the effect and after the effect has ceased to be ) "acts efficiently" (*Samyak Karoti*) in bringing about the effect, which itself then becomes the cause.

The perception or the experience of the "world" exists within the atomic particle of infinite Consciousness, but it is not in any way different from Consciousness. Like the mirror reflection which is not different from the mirror, the infinite Consciousness is itself the "creation". Creation exists wherever Consciousness is present and, therefore, *creation is truly uncreated.* The realization that I perceive creation whenever I am conscious, at any time at any place (and every human being can say this), transforms me (as the "I") from an infinitesimal particle of Consciousness into the infinite Consciousness itself. A drop on the surface of the ocean *is* the ocean itself.

The *jiva* (individual) perceives and experiences the external world with the externalized senses, and the inner world with the inner senses. When the experience of the external world is going on, the range of internal notions is vague and unspecific. When the mind is turned inwards the nature of reality is perceived with greater clarity.

In a gold bracelet there can be seen the substance that is the gold and the shape or appearance that is the bracelet. In the Self (Consciousness), there is the substance being the Consciousness and the notion being that of the phenomenal object.

The body appears as a concept or image in Consciousness, a notion entertained by Consciousness, and the identification of Consciousness with the body produces the corresponding personal consciousness or subtle body (*ativahika* or *puryashtaka*) composed of mind, intellect, the ego-sense and the five elements. While the infinite, universal Consciousness is formless, the personal consciousness moves from body to body in the process of evolution until it realizes its true nature of universality (enlightenment). Consciousness exists all the time, not only in the waking state, but also during dreaming and deep sleep states (because on waking up there is knowledge of dreams and deep sleep).

Consciousness exists equally in inanimate objects, insentient bodies (as in deep sleep) and in sentient bodies. The dream state in the sentient bodies is the experience of this creation, and its waking state is *truly* the transcendental (*turiya*) state of liberation while living. Beyond the *turiya* state is the state of universal, infinite Consciousness.

Any distinction, it must be constantly repeated, is only notional, made for the purpose of understanding the position. All there is, is Consciousness or Self or Noumenon, and the entire phenomenal manifestation is but the objective expression of its cosmic energy.

Descriptions of the creation of the universe are given in scriptures merely to make the matter easier for disciples to understand. When you have clearly understood what the illustrations and the words try to explain, they are to be thrown away. Thus it is said in Vedanta that the phenomenal manifestation is a natural expression of the cosmic energy (*chit-shakti*) of the infinite Consciousness or Brahman. Actually, in the infinite Consciousness there is neither the intention of the cosmic energy to express itself, nor any veil of delusion. The manifestation of the universe is just the objective expression of the subjective Absolute in which, as Subject, there is not the slightest touch of objectivity.

The Truth can be realized only when ignorance disappears, usually through instruction from those who are already enlightened. Such instruction needs the use of illustrations, descriptions, stories, and therefore words. It is all only *maya* playing a game of hide and seek. The infinite, universal Consciousness identifies itself with the individual form as the personal consciousness, and then the personal consciousness seeks its Source or True Nature! When the light of true knowledge arises, the darkness that was ignorance disappears. The real questions should be directed towards how to get rid of ignorance, not how the ignorance arose. Realization of the Truth comports the realization that ignorance is not a fact but illusion.

There is actually no division in Consciousness, no separation, that can be called "creation" or the "world". Such illusory "creation" emerges from nothing and ultimately dissolves into nothing. Its very nature is void, and therefore it does not exist. This is the Truth. That which did not exist in the beginning will not exist in the end, and even now it does not exist. This the Truth. This appearance of manifestation is like a dream, and the only reality, in which it appears and disappears, is the infinite Consciousness. No one is born, no one lives, no one dies. This is the Truth.

The notion that Consciousness appears as the universe, like the rope appears as the snake, is truly for the entertainment of the childish and the ignorant. The enlightened rest forever in that Truth which is changeless, in the direct awareness that there is none but the Self. When the qualities of the mind are lost, the essentials of the Infinite take over. When the mind vacates, the pure Consciousness takes over.

Creation exists as long as thought and conceptualization exist. Just as the essence of a thing exists in the thing, (i.e. oil in seeds, fragrance in flowers) the faculty of objective perception exists in the perceiver. Indeed, there can hardly be any distinction between the two (i.e. sugar and its sweetness, or a chili and its pungency).

Manifestation, in the totality of its sensorially perceptible aspects, is nothing other than Consciousness. "Mind" is the content of consciousness. But there should be no misunderstanding: Manifestation, in itself, is no thing at all. The objects therein are not "composed" of any sort of "mind-stuff", because they are just not there. Then what are the objects in the manifestation? They are purely apperceptions integral in their perceiving. The perception and perceiving are indeed the supposed "mind" that they are assumed to be. In other words, there is no "mind" as such. There is only apperceiving. "Mind" along with the concepts of "space" and "time" only apparently exist in order to render the manifestation perceptible.

Objectively speaking, the position is that there cannot possibly be anything apart from the phenomenon of perception; and perception, in the form of apperceiving, is totally devoid of any objective quality. *"Mind," therefore, is all that everything appears to be, but itself is nothing other than the apperceiving.* In other words, phenomena are whatever Consciousness is. Both are equally real and equally unreal. That which is created must necessarily be of the essence of that from which it was created. The immediate "cause" of the manifestation is the thought I Am, when Consciousness throbs into movement. Thus the manifested phenomena are of the nature of thought, objectivized in thought. Yet the phenomena (although imaginary) produce "realistic" effects of "realistic" causes, just as in a dream, an imagined sex act produces "realistic" results.

*Thus Consciousness is the creator. Mind (its content) is the instrument through which phenomena are created.* The perceived object is inherent in the perceiver. But let it never be forgotten that there never has been any creation or destruction. From the infinite potentiality emerges the infinite manifestation and it exists therein as the infinite — the one static, the other movement; the one unextended and formless, the other with form extended in space-time.

The infinite, universal Consciousness is the seed of the five elements; the five elements are the seed of the manifested universe. What results from the seed can only be of the nature of the seed. The manifested universe, therefore, is nothing but the unmanifest Absolute, the Consciousness — and there is no seed as such, because in this uncreated creation there is neither the seed nor its result. All there is is Consciousness in its subjectivity that precludes any need to know itself.

There never has been any entity as mind. It is nothing but Consciousness that exists, and what gives rise to the notions of mind and the universe (and all other allied notions) is all of the nature of Consciousness. When the very basis of the universe is an illusory notion, how can the "me" and the "you" be real? There never have been any causative factors and so never could there have been any creation. At the level of the infinite Consciousness, whatever appears as phenomenal manifestation is a reflection of Consciousness. Reality, infinite and changeless, is nothing other than Consciousness. *Consciousness as sentience enables sentient objects to experience the senses and their objects. Consciousness as mind-intellect enables human beings to think and discriminate.*

The transcendental Reality is What-Is. The world is not unreal inasmuch as Reality is immanent therein. What is false is the mind which is the separating, limiting notion that creates a division between the "me" and the world. What appears within Consciousness as its own reflection — the manifestation of the universe — is not separate or different from Consciousness. While the shadow, *by itself*, has no existence and is therefore unreal, the shadow is not different from the substance *when seen together*. When there is no mind in operation, when there is no conceptualizing, it is clearly known, felt, experienced, that phenomenality is only the objective expression of the subjective noumenon. The substance and its shadow, the ocean and the waves, the sugar and its sweetness cannot be separated. Any separation is only notional, made merely for the purpose of intellectual understanding.

The phenomenal "creation" is nothing other than Consciousness, and *Consciousness alone is aware of this creation.* When thought-words concerning "creation" subside into irrelevance, the true meaning of "creation" is at once *sensed* as the eternal Consciousness itself; the word "Consciousness" includes "creation," and the word "creation" is included in the comprehension of "Consciousness." Of course, when there is apperception (pure knowledge), the question of comprehension does not arise, because then there is no comprehender to comprehend anything — the comprehender has to be annihilated before there can be apperception.

God is not Shiva or Vishnu or Brahma, nor the sun or the moon or the wind or the fire or the water. God is that formless subjectivity, pure potential, the infinite, universal Consciousness which alone exists even after the cosmic dissolution. It is only within this pure, infinite Consciousness, the potential plenum, that phenomenal manifestation arose as a mere reflection of that potentiality, as a mere objective expression of that pure subjectivity.

The phenomenal objectivization of this pure subjectivity appears and functions in our *outer* world of consciousness in the waking state, precisely like sentient and insentient objects seem to exist and function in the *inner* world of consciousness in the dream state. Nothing really happens in either state. Consciousness is the substance and substratum in both objectivizations — the dream world and the apparently "real" world. Both are objective manifestations in Consciousness, when Consciousness is in movement.

The external worship of a form as God is prescribed only for those whose psyches have not been sufficiently purified and whose intuitive intelligence has not been adequately awakened. Such worship of an object created by themselves as a concept may give the worshippers a certain amount of satisfaction and peace of mind but it is a futile process from the point of view of experiencing one's true nature.

The God who is fit to be worshipped by the highly evolved intellects is one which supports the entire phenomenal creation as its substance...A God beyond all concepts, infinite and intemporal...A God which, like the flavor in food, is within every sentient being and therefore needs no seeking...A God who cannot be comprehended because He transcends the mind and five senses of cognition.

Universal Consciousness is to be worshipped by one's own personal consciousness, not by offering flowers or food or sandalpaste, nor by lighting incense and waving lights. It should be worship without any effort, by self-realization alone, by the supreme meditation in the continuous, unbroken awareness of the within, the indwelling presence. This worship needs no effort because there is nothing to be attained which one does not already possess.

Worship of the universal Consciousness consists of accepting wholeheartedly whatever comes our way unsought and unsolicited — all physical pleasures and all ailments. It is accepting whatever activities take place through the psychophysical organism. The Self should be worshipped with all of the pleasures that come effortlessly and spontaneously, whether such pleasures are sanctioned or forbidden by the scriptures, whether considered desirable or undesirable, appropriate or inappropriate. The Self should be worshipped with all experiences, whether beautiful and pleasant or ugly and unpleasant, that arise due to the coincidence of time, circumstance and environment. Experiences should be accepted in a state of equanimity, like the openness of space, with the mind utterly quiescent in infinite expansion within. External actions take place without volition, without desire or rejection. All is witnessed without desire, without rejection, without judging.

# BOOK TWO

*The Individual in Relation to the*
*Phenomenal Manifestation*

# The Individual's Problem

The traditional conditioning of the "sea of *samsara*" is so strong that you are compelled to seek the state of *nirvana* from an outside source. You pray: "I am drowning in this ocean of misery, O Lord, please save me." Then you are told that liberation is not all that easy or simple, that you must make long and arduous efforts before you can attain liberation. Various paths with names and rites and regulations are prescribed. Then you are told that you are not bound at all, and that, therefore, the question of freedom does not arise. However, all this is happening to a "you"; this is being told to "you."

Is it not simpler, and more direct, to understand at once that there is no "you" at all, that the "you" is a concept created by the mind. "You" are an illusion. In such understanding there is no conceptualizing, no mind acting as the comprehender ego — "you." Such understanding, without any "you" as the comprehender, is pure understanding or apperception. Such apperception — or, rather, such apperceiving — is all that there *Is*: Consciousness, or Awareness, or God, or whatever you may call it, whose only "doing" is witnessing (without any judgement) the entire functioning of the total manifestation.

The earlier stages are parts of the circle which gets completed only with the final annihilation of the "you" or "me."

# The Concept Of Bondage

In order to understand clearly the relationship between the human being and the phenomenal world, it is necessary to notionally bifurcate it as the perceived or the objective aspect, and the perceiving or subjective aspect. It must be stressed that such a distinction is purely notional (though significant), because although they appear as dual in manifestation, they are not so when unmanifested.

In regard to the perceived or the objective aspect (the apparent aspect), sentient beings appear in the manifestation like all other phenomena in the apparent universe. There is, objectively, no difference between animate and inanimate objects — all are objects arising concurrently in the phenomenal manifestation. This is the perceived or objective aspect.

The difference (notional) arises from the point of view of the apparent universe *being known* to sentient beings through their sentience, by means of the senses. Sentience is that aspect of manifestation through which phenomena (including other sentient objects) are cognized. In other words, if appearance is seen as the static aspect of manifestation, sentience is seen as the dynamic aspect. Through sentience the senses and the faculties of cognition do the cognitive interpretation. To this extent there is a difference between animate and inanimate objects: *while both are perceived objects, only an animate object can do the perceiving itself.*

It is because of the perceiving or *subjective aspect* of the manifestation in Consciousness that the human being considers himself to be a separate, independent and autonomous entity with choice of decision and action. It is because he forgets the perceived or objective aspect of his own appearance as a part of the total manifestation that the misconception arises. Despite all appearances to the contrary, the human being, like all other sentient beings, is objectively nothing more than a phantom, a dream figure. He is activated as utterly and totally as puppets are activated by the puppeteer. All that the human being does is pure conceptualizing through the production of illusory images and interpretations by means of the relevant psychosomatic mechanism known as the body.

All phenomenal "existence" is hypothetical. Each and every action is dreamed or imagined by a Dreamer that has no objective quality whatever, that is to say, by Consciousness in its subjective aspect. Whatever is objectively cognizable is a dreamed fantasy of living. "We" are only the dreamed figures, the phenomenal objects in the living dream of the dreaming subject, the Consciousness which, *as such*, is itself a concept. A clear and profound understanding of this situation is awakening or enlightenment.

*The entire problem of living arises because the human being assumes the subjective aspect in his objective capacity* and draws upon himself all the "suffering" that is purely imaginary. A realization, that it is as the *subjective aspect of Consciousness* that the human being dreams the universe by objectivizing it, means awakening from the living dream — or, enlightenment. The dream is seen to be without any cause. This is the final Truth.

## The Ubiquitous "Who"

It is not too difficult to acquire intellectually the basic understanding that we are the immanent substance and not the "fleeting and tormented shadow." What is indeed uncommon is to reach the totality of this understanding intuitively. The reason is that the understanding is not generally accepted *as such* but only with a "who" attached to it. The verb is not accepted without a subject, the event not without the *conceived* individual. To put it a little differently, *the illusory character of everything in the universe is understood and accepted. Everything that is except the illusory character of the one who understands and accepts it!* It is almost impossible to accept the total annihilation of an identity that has been hammered into existence by continual conditioning.

Thus there is a block to the total understanding. The block is the ubiquitous "who." And unless the "who" — or the "one" or the "me" — disappears completely, there cannot arise that non-intellectual understanding, that intuitive apprehension, that profound and absolute conviction, that luminous apperception which needs no support from scriptures or otherwise.

The "me" demands to be present at any enquiry concerning "himself" and the nature of the phenomenal manifestation. It is not unlike a blind man who wants to understand the nature of the world around him but only on the basis that it exist in the darkness to which he is subjected. A real difficulty arises whenever one listens to a *guru*, or reads a book, adumbrating metaphysical truths (adumbrating or pointing is all that can be done) since the words are inevitably addressed to an individual! Even the *mahavakya* "That Thou Art" is addressed to a "thou". It is as if the individual is never allowed to forget that he is an individual even though he is repeatedly told that no individual can exist as an independent, autonomous entity!

It is because of this Gordian knot — our conditioning prevents the understanding, yet without this *basic* under-

standing enlightenment cannot take place — that the path
has been described as the pathless path that leads no body
from no "here" to no "there!" There can not be any
unknotting of this Gordian knot. It can only be cut
asunder by a sudden, spontaneous, unequivocal *acceptance* of the understanding without any deliberate attempt
to understand that understanding. Why? Because *we are
that understanding.* Instead of demanding, like the blind
man, an understanding of the world on the basis of eternal
darkness, why not accept what is stated, with such fer-
vent urgency, by the Buddha (and scores of such others in
every part of the world) that there is no such thing as a
"self", a separate "individual", a "being"?

Still, the question arises "who" says so? "Who" is
writing this? No one, of course. There never has been a
"who" from the beginning of time, except *the "Who" that
is phenomenally ubiquitous and noumenally utterly absent!*
The one who asks the question is the "Who", that is the
seeker, seeking Himself. It is for this reason that Nisargadatta Maharaj repeatedly asserted that he is not an
individual speaking to another individual, but *Consciousness* speaking to Consciousness.

There is a fact that is not generally recognized, a fact
that is not easily acceptable even if it is realized intellectually. This fact is that an object is known as an object
because, and only because, there is a reaction of one or
more senses of a sentient being to an outside stimulus.
That is to say, there is a stimulus which appears to derive
from sources external to the psychosomatic mechanism,
the re-agent apparatus. Objects would not be known as
objects if there were no reactions of the senses of sentient
beings to a variety of outside stimuli — which means, of
course, that *apart from the re-agent apparatus through which
the objects are surmised, objects, as such, have no demonstrable
existence.*

The subject which cognizes objects is itself an object to
other sentient objects. Thus, the rather obvious facts is
that all sentient objects — each acting as subject of the
other objects — are merely a surmise. The factual exist-

ence of neither the object nor the subject can be demonstrated. What this really means is that there is no acceptable evidence for the existence of a phenomenal world external to and independent of the consciousness of sentient beings. To carry the point logically further, the external world would thus seem to be nothing other than the sentient beings who are the cognizers of this world. But the sentient beings themselves do not seem to have any independent external existence (either as subject or object) and must therefore be a concept in the Consciousness in which they are cognized! It would thus appear that all objects — as subject or object — including the sentient beings are nothing but Consciousness! Finally, Consciousness itself has no demonstrable existence and must therefore be a conceptual assumption.

The only conclusion to which we seem to have arrived logically is that consciousness must be regarded as the manifested aspect of the unmanifest — the ultimate concept to point towards That which by definition is inconceivable. Beyond that we cannot go because conceptuality cannot arise out of conceptuality but only out of what is non-conceptual. What is conceived as being objectively present can only arise from what is objectively absent, manifestation from what is unmanifest. Just as an eye cannot see itself as an object, conceptuality cannot conceive or objectify itself. In other words, Consciousness (in which conceptuality arises) is *pure* non-conceptuality, not tainted either by the conceptual or the non-conceptual. It is an absolute absence of both positive and negative conceptuality and thus an absolute absence of name and form. It does not exist as an object. It is *the ultimate absence from which appears all presence.*

It is essential to understand that Consciousness does not *project* the phenomenal universe — it *is* the phenomenal universe, manifested as its objective self:
" 'I' *do not exist objectively, but the phenomenally objectivized universe is 'my' self.*"

Apart from pure Consciousness, nothing exists independently — neither the senses nor the mind, nor their objects. It is Consciousness alone which appears as the senses within an individual and as the various objects without. And as the mind it gives an interpretation to the objects outside as acceptable and not acceptable.

The pure Consciousness that is infinite and eternal is ever free from all modifications. In Vedantic terms, the *jiva* (the individual) is merely a notion that arises simultaneously and spontaneously along with the notion "I Am". It is this notional, personal consciousness that lives and moves and believes itself to be the individual entity. With the arising of the I-am-ness, Consciousness is known as the ego (*ahamkara*); with the arising of thoughts it is known as mind (*manas*); with the arising of awareness it is known as intelligence (*buddhi*). All in all nothing exists except Consciousness in its various aspects — as the body, as the senses, as the ego, as thoughts, as the intellect and as the objects outside. It is through the incredibly quick repetitions of these notions that the personal consciousness (the subtle personality) condenses itself into apparently material solidity or substantiality. The same Consciousness thereafter identifies itself with each individual object in separation. When this self-delusion disappears, the Consciousness becomes aware of its universality and infinity — and this is what is known as "enlightenment."

All the bodies (*puryashtaka*) arise in Consciousness as images — whether it is an object as near as a chair or as distant as a star — precisely like the manifestation of the entire universe (the first or original *puryashtaka*) arose in the infinite Consciousness. The *jiva* (individual) sees as objects whatever it conceives from the viewpoint of that part of memory with which it was infused at the moment of conception. Just as the cosmic elements evolve in the macrocosm, in a similar manner, the corresponding senses evolve in the microcosm. Of course, it must be constantly borne in mind, while trying to understand the mechanics of the apparent process of manifestation, that *nothing has actually been "created."* All that appears is mind-stuff of which all dreams are made. When the illusion of the mirage is understood, the notion that water actually exists in the mirage automatically vanishes. Still, the idea of water was necessary to explain the illusion.

Only the Self or Consciousness exists. Everything else, the *jiva*, the *puryashtaka* (the subtle body) and all the rest of the notions necessary to explain the illusion of manifestation vanish when the entire subject is clearly appreciated. However, the enquiry into the nature of the several notions (including the individual *jiva*) was indeed the enquiry into their unreality.

Consciousness identifies itself with each object, assumes the nature of the individual, and experiences what the individual thinks. Knowledge is inherent in Consciousness — indeed, they are the same precisely as space and void are identical. But, in its identification with the individual *jiva*, knowledge — the I-am-ness — gets divided into subject/object relationship so that the multitude of objects get notionally limited by space and time. This limitation is the result of notional division as consciousness/knowledge, consciousness/mind, subject/object. But subjective knowledge, pure knowledge, is the very essence of Consciousness and to That it always returns. When the superimposed false is seen as false, the real is exposed as having always been there.

The fictitious movement of energy in Consciousness is what the "mind" is, and the natural expressions of the mind (like the hissing of a snake or the roar of a tiger) are known as thoughts or ideas. *Consciousness plus conceptualization is thought. Consciousness minus conceptualization is our true nature, What-We-Are.* Consciousness plus conceptualization gives rise to the dualism "me" and "not-me". There cannot be any conceptualization without the "me" which is the very basis of conceptualization. It is conceptualization which limits the universal Consciousness into a personal consciousness or mind, or ego. This is how the ego arises. The very understanding in depth of the apparent difference between the universal Consciousness which is What-We-Are, and the personal consciousness which is what-we-appear-to-be, starts the process of reversing back and inwards to our true nature. The apperception of our true nature stops the outward flow of thought based on the conceptual welfare of the conceptual "me", and leads to the phenomenon known as enlightenment. This *happens* suddenly, spontaneously and effortlessly. It is not expected at all. Indeed, any expectation would be an obstacle.

As long as certain notions persist, the correlated assumption of bondage (and the pain and sorrow associated with that assumption) must continue to plague the supposed individual. The human being is not "something *that is*". It is a phenomenon. As a phenomenon, as an appearance in someone's consciousness, the human being is only "something that *seems to be*."

The whole point of bondage is that that which cognizes an appearance (the "me") wrongly assumes that it is the subject of that cognition and thus is an entity separate from that which is cognized. The fact of the matter, however, is that that which cognizes and that which is cognized are both appearances in each other's consciousness. Indeed, every conceivable thing that our senses perceive and our mind cognizes (through the interpretation of what is perceived by the senses) cannot be anything other than an appearance in Consciousness, objectified and interpreted as an event in space-time.

What is to be understood is that both the assumptions and the bondage based on these assumptions are merely phenomenal and therefore only apparent. Such understanding at once demolishes the psychological elements of the purely psychological bondage, and thereafter what remains is merely the psychological conditioning brought about by that apparent bondage. This conditioning will be wiped out by a de-conditioning process consisting of the concept of "reality" being replaced by the concept of "appearance". Such a de-conditioning process — dissolving as it does that which was misconstrued as "real" and "separate" — must necessarily dissolve the spurious cognizing entity. Both are then seen as appearances in Consciousness, obviously without any independence or autonomy.

There is truly no diversity in creation. Diversity is merely an appearance in Consciousness, according to the notions that appear in a particular personal consciousness during evolution (or involution, if you will). Many of the notions intermingle, and thus, through permutations and combinations, an infinite variety is produced in this diversity. But, the diversity appears only in the one infinite, universal Consciousness.

Actions taking place through existing body mind organisms at any given moment produce certain reactions in the future. These reactions get reflected as future actions through newly created individual organisms. These in their turn create further results and so the cause-effect relationship continues through the creation of fresh characters in this unfinished play that is this life and living in our world. Evolution brings about a succession of "lives" in a progression towards the ultimate phenomenon known as enlightenment. In this state, no mnemonic expectations remain unfulfilled and no new volitional expectations are created. But in this process of evolution — beginning from a sense of dissatisfaction with material and sensorial pleasures, then passing through dispassion, on towards self-enquiry, and culminating in the total abdication and surrender of volition and identification that ultimately means enlightenment — no individual entity is involved. It is not an individual entity that is born and reborn. All that happens is a gradual progress through several lives — though *not of any particular entity* — towards the ultimate disidentification of the universal Consciousness from the particular physical form, with which it had identified itself as personal consciousness, or mind.

Bondage for the supposed individual appears because of a mistaken identity. What-We-Are is the animating Consciousness — which is noumenon. What we *think* we are is the phenomenal object to which the animating Consciousness provides sentience. The only "existence" any phenomenal object, including the human being, can have is merely apparent. That is to say, it is only an appearance in Consciousness, an objectivization that is entirely dependent for its existence on the mind that objectivizes it. In other words, the existence of the phenomenal object, with mind as its only nature (like any dreamed character), cannot possibly have any independent nature of its own.

This mistaken identity of a separate "me" arises when the impersonal Consciousness comes into manifestation by objectifying itself as subject and object, and at once becomes identified with each object. In this process of personalizing Consciousness and thinking of It as "me", we thereby make the one and only subject ("I") into an object. "I" is the direct expression of subjectivity, totally devoid of the essentially objective "me". This objectivizing of the pure subjectivity of "I" and understanding it as "me" is precisely what constitutes "bondage". In fact this conceptual "me" is itself the supposed bondage from which "liberation" is sought.

It is ignorance which makes the body and its movements seem different from and independent of the mind (consciousness). Actually, it is the mind which creates within itself the appearance of the body, like a potter creates a pot out of wet clay.

The mind gets involved in the phenomenal manifestation, (its own creation), by entertaining notions such as "I am happy" or "I am miserable". The Consciousness (of which mind is the content) regains its universality when there is realization of the falseness or illusoriness of all that is sensorially perceptible. Then, peace and equanimity prevail.

It is the universal Consciousness alone that is. Consciousness is like a vast ocean on the surface of which arise waves of different shapes and sizes. If waves could think like sentient human beings, the small wave would think it is small and the big one that it is big. One would think it is warm, another that it is cold, and the wave that is about to be broken up by the wind would think that it is dying! The point is that waves are mere *appearances* on the surface of the ocean. All is really water.

The silkworm weaves its cocoon and then binds itself within. The universal Consciousness creates the millions of sentient beings as part of the total manifestation, and then binds itself within each form by identification as a separate being. In fact there is neither bondage nor liberation. There is only the play of the infinite, universal Consciousness which, by identification, considers itself bound. Then, by disidentifying itself through self-enquiry, it considers itself liberated. It is a game of hide and seek that Consciousness plays with Itself, within Itself.

The question of 'bondage' and 'freedom' can arise only if the true nature of the "individual" has not been well and truly understood. When there is a clear realization of the fundamental fact that the individual is the manifest appearance of the unmanifest, the question of bondage cannot arise. The question cannot arise for the simple reason that the questioner does not truly exist except as an appearance in Consciousness, a movement in the mind.

Whatever the mechanism of phenomenality — apparent causality or the more scientifically acceptable system of statistical probability — the fact remains that the individual, as such, is merely an appearance in Consciousness. It is a psyche-soma obviously incapable of exercising freedom of any kind.

That which thinks it is in bondage is that which thinks it is a psyche-soma subject to causality. Phenomenally in a psyche-soma there is no "ens" to have any kind of freedom. But that which thinks it is in bondage (or free) is identified in thought with a phenomenal object and *appears* to be subject to bondage or (freedom). This leads us to the ineluctable conclusion that "he" (the psyche-soma which thinks of itself as a separate entity) who thinks he is free is as much in bondage as "he" who considers himself bound.

To that subjective "being" of which all phenomenal manifestation is an appearance, no concept at all can apply because all concepts are the product of duality.

The relationship between Consciousness and the body is purely conceptual. The phenomenal world, including the body, may be said to have been fancied into creation by Consciousness precisely as a dream world is created during sleep. The illusory entity gets objectified when Consciousness uses its own creative energy to bring into conceptual existence the multitude of "me's" by identifying itself with—and thus limiting itself to—each of the bodies so created.

Truly, neither the body, nor the Consciousness undergoes any experience either of pleasure or of pain. It is only the ignorant mind that suffers, and the mind is the content of Consciousness. It is only in the condition of sleep that dreams arise (not the condition of deep sleep) and dreams disappear when the waking condition arises. It is only in ignorance that the mind dreams of world appearance. When the ignorance disappears through the awakening of knowledge — when the light of knowledge dispels the darkness of ignorance — the world appearance (and all it contains) is seen as the illusion that it is. So, *what suffers the experience of pleasure and misery is neither the body nor the universal Consciousness, but that which is known by various names such as personal consciousness, mind, ego, ignorance, mental conditioning etc.*

Our unhappiness and suffering (our supposed "bondage") is entirely the effect of the identification of What-We-Are (the animating Consciousness) with the subject or perceiver-cognizer element in our division into subject and object, perceiver and perceived. This identification leads to the conceptual transformation of that subject element into a supposedly independent and autonomous individual entity who can exercise personal volition in choice, decision and action.

The fact, however, remains that *the subject element and the object element are interdependent and mutually inseparable* in mind. The two together constitute the functioning of the event and clearly neither could have any sort of personal volition or autonomy in any circumstances.

It is this illusory identification, leading to an illusory entitification which is the cause of all the supposed bondage. What-We-Are (Consciousness-at-rest or Whole-Mind, or Noumenon) can have no existence *as such*. We can exist only as objective manifestation of the totality of phenomena. We — *as the subjective noumenon* — cannot, in other words, have any objective existence and therefore cannot be subject either to constraint or to liberation therefrom. Our "bondage" and the associated misery and suffering can have only a conceptual and illusory basis.

When the universal Consciousness manifested itself as the universe, the characteristic tendencies of each sentient being simultaneously came into existence. The embodied *jiva* was "born" with its own *dharma* or natural characteristics. There is no basic difference between thought and action. Action is essentially the movement of energy in Consciousness and becomes the cause of the inevitable effect in the inexorable law of causality. When such action comes to an end, conceptualization too ceases, and *in the absence of conceptualization there is no action*. This is clearly seen in the case of the liberated sages.

The sole reality is infinite Consciousness. Everything else is a concept, beginning with the primal thought (concept) I Am, by which Consciousness viewed itself as the object of perception in the duality of subject and object (and all the innumerable pairs of interrelated opposites).

Pure movement in Consciousness is *karma* or action untainted by individual or personal volition. When such action is pursued because of mnemonic impressions of past pleasures, it leads to the supposed bondage.

The impure mind, tainted by the dualism of "me and not-me" pollutes all relationships and creates suspicion and enmity all around. The same event that is experienced by several people is interpreted in different ways according to the state of the mind. In fact *what a man thinks he is, is nothing but the mind itself*. Indeed, it is the mind creating objects within itself that is able to turn Consciousness away from its true nature and make it identify itself with the body. It is mind which appears as wind that moves the leaves on the tree...as the solidity of the earth...the void in the sky...the luminosity in the luminous.

The senses are born of the mind. It is not that the mind and thoughts arise because of the senses. If "the mind is elsewhere", one is unaware of what is right in front. One is unaware of the taste of what is being eaten. One is even unaware of pain until it reaches a degree that brings the mind back. And that which is able to apperceive this and understand this must necessarily be different in nature from what is perceived.

It is the wanting to "become", the wanting of change from What-Is, that is the cause of the supposed sorrow. The Self (Consciousness) is totally different in nature from the body-mind, as different as the lotus is from the water. So long as the inert body-mind continues to pursue illusory pleasure, so long will the darkness of illusion continue. But as soon as the mind turns inward, towards the light of awakening, the darkness of the ignorance disappears at once.

It appears as if the sky is polluted by dust, but the sky is not affected by the particles of dust floating about. Pleasure and pain appear to be experienced by "oneself", but they affect neither the body nor the Self which transcends everything while being immanent therein.

The phenomenal manifestation is but the reflection of the unmanifest within itself. They are nondual. Therefore there is no sorrow, no delusion; no creation, no destruction; no birth, no death; whatever is, *is*.

What is to be done? Nothing.

Then what happens? "You", then, are free of the dualism of "me" and "not me". "You" are at peace *within*, without any sorrow or doubt in mind. "You" remain firmly established in the inner silence, without any concern for your welfare, content with whatever comes along. "You" live effortlessly, without either wanting anything or deliberately giving up anything. This is brought about by the firm apprehension that everything happens in

Consciousness without any effort by any supposed individual entity, precisely as a mirror reflects the objects around it without any intention. A flight of birds is reflected in the water of the lake but the birds do not *intend* to make a reflection, nor does the water *intend* to reflect the flight of the birds.

When the apperception of Truth occurs, it is realized that whatever comes one's way unsought must be wholeheartedly accepted and enjoyed. Nothing need be abandoned or rejected or given up, because even such renunciation would be volitional. It is realized that while there is nothing to work for, this does not imply deliberate inaction, because deliberate action and inaction are identical *When the mind ceases to entertain any notion of doership or non-doership, all action becomes non-action.*

When most people speak of God or divinity they generally mean the inevitable, the unknown beyond their supposed control and beyond the events of natural order. They pray for the acceptable to happen and the unacceptable not to happen. Others refer to God or divine grace as that which brings about equanimity and the cessation of the fleeting joy and sorrow.

In actual fact the supposed individual functions in this world strictly according to the providential dictates of the natural order (*niyati* or *prajnya*) or, just as the wind moves in space. Still, the individual may consider his actions as volitional actions based on his personal choice and decision. The movement of plants and trees along a mountain slope makes it appear as if it is the peak that is swaying. Similarly, it is because of the prompting of nature that the supposed individual acts or refrains from acting. It is not out of his supposed volition as an autonomous and independent entity. All such action — or lack of action — is wholly within the totality of functioning in manifestation, and is nothing but a movement in Consciousness.

So long as there is conceptualization, there is the individual and God, and whatever else is objectivized in the mind. When mind is vacant and conceptualization has ceased, there is no one to be concerned with anything. Why should there be any fear or worry about the conceptual void? Who is to be afraid — and of what?

Bondage, to which the individual considers himself subject, is nothing but attachment to an illusory volition. It is attachment to a supposed "will", which is to be translated as the exercise of an independent, personal choice of decision and action by that illusory entity with which What-One-Is is identified and which is called "me".

What this means is that the pronoun "I" is used quite incorrectly. "I" is, basically and fundamentally, the eternal subject without the slightest touch of objectivity. Yet, the pronoun is used for a phenomenal objectivization as if it were perfectly free to do whatever it wished, whenever and wherever it so wished. But the simple and incontrovertible fact is that an objectivization, like any other piece of a mechanism can do nothing of itself.

What has in fact happened is that the driver of a motor car has identified himself with the car, and thereafter considers the car as "me". This assumed personality of the " me-mechanism" is a concept, factually nonexistent. This is what causes conflict, suffering and bondage. There is the need to function volitionally, as against the deepest intuitive conviction that the entity (supposed to exercise his volition) does not, can not, exist.

When the incongruity of this situation is firmly understood, the illusion of a suffering entity in bondage at once disappears. "I" returns to its original subjectivity when the eclipse of the "me" disappears. What lives (or, more correctly "is lived") sensorially, is the object, and What-I-Am is its sentience. What-I-Am expresses itself as phenomenal functioning — seeing, hearing, tasting — but there is no objective "I" (the "me" is a fiction) that sees, hears, tastes. Only the object suffers and "I" am not an object.

The infinite Consciousness is all there is, and there is no relationship between mind and Consciousness except like fragrance to the flower. *The senses are inert and insentient and merely act as channels through which mind flows out*

*to reach objective experiences.* The eyes see objects but the
notions of the experience being pleasant or otherwise arise
not in the eyes but in the mind. Thus the sense functions
themselves are innocent. Of course, without them, the
functioning as such — seeing, smelling, tasting, touching,
hearing — could not take place. If the mind keeps itself
aloof from the sense functions which are natural, there
would be no suffering. It is this illusory relationship
between mind and senses which produces notions, like
lust and anger, that lead to unhappiness and bondage.

It is only ignorance which brings about a false sense of
cause and effect between senses and their objects, the
experiences and the illusory experiencer, actions and their
illusory do-er. Where does the error lie? How does it
arise? Whose is the error? The sequence actually is something like this: trees grow, and provide timber, pieces of
timber are tied together by ropes made of fibres, the
blacksmith fashions the axe which the carpenter uses to
build a house — and he builds the house not to live in, but
to earn a livelihood! In other words, events in this world
happen independently of one another and their connection with one another, or cause and effect, is illusory or
accidental. There is the classic instance of the ripe coconut
falling "because of" the alighting of a crow on the branch.
Can anyone be blamed? When apperception happens,
error remains an error by itself, knowledge becomes
knowledge, the real is seen as real, the unreal as unreal,
what has been destroyed is destroyed, and what remains,
remains. There is no need of any searching for cause and
effect, no question of guilt or achievement.

When understanding dawns, conceptualization ceases
and mind becomes vacant. The very nature of the mind
is ignorance and therefore stupidity. When the mind
stops (conceptualization ceases), peace or wisdom
prevails. No thought of either happiness or unhappiness
diverts the equanimity of the pure mind.

## Experiences And Awareness

"Experience" is what is experienced on reacting to an outside stimulus or to an event. It is not factual but conceptual. It is this fact that is very often ignored: that experience as such has no existence. The reaction is sensually interpreted as pleasant or unpleasant, and such reaction will vary from person to person, and even for the same person, the reaction will vary according to the circumstances. Indeed, *if for some reason there is no reaction, there will be no experience at all.*

Together with the fact that experience is conceptual and not factual, the other basic fact is that in the absence of the "me" there cannot be any experience, any cognizance. And *vice versa*, there must be an experience whenever there seems to be an awareness of "me". In other words, both the "experience" and the "me" are conceptual and there cannot be one without the other, and of course being conceptual, an experience is always in context of "time". In the present moment, *now*, there is no horizontal stringing-together of consecutive moments into duration. *Now* there is neither the "me" nor the "experience".

It is essential to distinguish between *an experience* and *experience-ing*. A "self" or "me" who considers itself autonomous, and "lives" and "dies" is a part of the temporal fantasy. In the fantasy there are the see-er, think-er, do-er, and the things seen (or sensorially perceived), thoughts and deeds. These "entities" are merely *figurants* in the temporal fantasy. The functioning that is implied — the doing as distinguished from the do-er and the deed — is not a conceptual interpretation of a precept but perceive-*ing*, which is the subjective aspect of What-We-Are. Therefore, "think-*ing*" and "feel-*ing*", not interpreted as thought and emotion by a "me", are still non-objective and impersonal. Since they are not being apparently experienced by an experiencer, they are the experience-*ing* which is all that "we" can be. It is the "Within" that is the source of all function-*ing*. It is the immutable background of the phenomenal process of "living" when not subjected to sequential duration. Experience of the "me" — positive or negative — is in duration, and is interpreted as thought and emotion, pleasure/pain, love/hate.

Why is this so? This is so because for experience to be individualized, there has to be an individual phenomenal object. This is why a philosopher like Schroedinger could say that Consciousness is a singular of which the plural is unknown. But a mystic like Nisargadatta Maharaj would insist that Consciousness is not a "singular" either. In other words, we cannot exist as conscious and rational entities, nor can we not-exist, because absence of positive existence comports also absence of its interrelated counterpart. *What-We-Are is the experience-ing but not the experience that is experienced by a "me"*.

What-We-Are, What-I-Am, cannot be conscious or aware because it *is* Consciousness or Awareness. It is impossible to be conscious of that which is being conscious or to be aware of that which is being aware. If I am aware of what I am, then what I am is the object of a subject that is aware of an object — and would thus be an object of which a subject is aware, and so on in a perpetual regression. What can be conscious or aware is a divided mind which can reason but cannot apperceive its own wholeness. But then, if there were only one man in the world, would he need to know he was a "man" — does light need to know that it is light?

# What Does Truth Imply In Practice?

It is perfectly axiomatic (but rarely accepted) that there cannot be any factuality as an entity (because no object has any self-nature or "own-being") and that therefore we cannot exist at all.

A sentient being is merely an image in mind, an appearance perceived and conceived by the "subject" of each such objectification. It is not "we" who do the perceiving and conceiving for there is no "we". "We" and "they" are perceived, conceived and interpreted through or via one another. This clearly means that there has to be a single source of perceiving which perceives through the multiple instruments of perceiving which are "ourselves". Each such instrument is conceived as an apparent entity, but really has no personal existence of its own.

If this fact is squarely faced, the conclusion is ineluctable that objectively we cannot be anything but what is perceived, conceived and interpreted through other sentient beings. The interpretation of the phenomenal objects that we are, will depend on whether it is done by our "friends" or "foes" or by "ourselves". The fact, however, remains that we are totally devoid of objective existence. What we are in life is merely an appearance in mind or consciousness. We have no fixed identity, quality or attributes.

It is important to note that subjectively also we are totally devoid of identity, quality or attributes, representing phenomenally that noumenal, subjective "I", the source of all phenomenality and manifestation.

The significant point that arises at this stage is: if, as ourselves, we are nothing, if we do not exist as autonomous entities, for whom is all this being said? The answer is, (as Nisargadatta Maharaj repeatedly asseverated), it is universal Consciousness speaking to the identified Consciousness. The understanding can never be at a personal level. When the understanding happens without any comprehender, there is a clear indication of What-We-Are through understanding what-we-are-not.

The fact remains that we are *apparent* entities living our lives. But the apperception of Truth brings about a recognition of the dual nature of living in this world which is based on relativity. And this recognition is what is required. It is the recognition that while our phenomenal limitations as an autonomous, separate entity, is illusory as *limitation*, our phenomenality is not illusory. It is inherent in our noumenality. In other words, we recognize the dual character of our "living" which is based on relativity, the comparison of opposing concepts. Thereafter, we live *as if* the world were real, as in a Punch and Judy show, as in a drama, as in a dream — merely witnessing the show.

It is for this reason that Maharaj used to say so often "understanding is all". A clear understanding (apperception) comports the conviction that, as mere appearances, we cannot possibly have any volition concerning choice or action. What then happens? What then happens is that "we" flow with the tide. All that remains is the flow of noumenal witnessing (without any phenomenal witnesses), the subjective element in our "living". Then, the living dream is dreamed in equanimity to its very end, until the phenomenal object drops.

# The Nature Of Existence

What does one really mean by "existence"? Unless we clearly understand what we mean when we use a particular word, considerable *avoidable* confusion will arise. It is a common experience that in discussions indefinite locutions (words) are used which have an affective implication which necessitates a volitional discrimination between pairs of mutually contradictory concepts. If this fact is firmly kept in mind, most of the infructuous discussions would be avoided.

"Existence", for instance, can have meaning only relative to "non-existence" because "existence" is a conceptual objectivization of some object that is, or appears to be. Other than that, in the abstract (not objectively applied) it has no meaning. If this were not so, if "existence" were not intended to mean specifically *"appears to have being"*, it would imply that there was no difference between an object and its appearance. But that would be an obvious contradiction in terms for "appears to be" would bring in its opposite "does not appear to be", and this would need potential non-apparent existence!

The significance of this analysis is that both existence and non-existence — both positive and negative existence — are conceptual modes of existence. It is the *absence of both*, the absence of conceptualizing itself, that is the in-seeing, that is the truth. In other words, any kind of existence is conceptual and therefore phenomenal. Only the absence of both positive and negative phenomenal presence through mutual annihilation is noumenal presence. For the whole-mind to function as totality, the split-mind must vacate and be in abeyance. And then such whole-mind functioning being phenomenally *negative* cannot be revealed through dualistic thought or verbal expression.

Similarly, *"living" as existence is a spatial illusion, while "dying" as non-existence is a temporal illusion* . What-we-think-we-are is a spatio-temporal illusion in a "living" based on the serializing of three-dimensional "stills" or "quanta". As with motion picture "stills", these are perceived and cognized as a movement only so long as the light of consciousness is available. When the light of consciousness gets shut off, we no longer "exist" because we are no longer elaborated in space and extended in duration. This is known as "dying". It is the apperception of the space-time mechanism as purely conceptual — noumenal understanding — which comports the annihilation of all conceptualizing. Then the truth of What-We-Are is revealed. *As What-We-Are, we have never lived and we cannot die.*

It is for this reason that the Masters have always declared that we neither exist nor do not exist. Existence — positive or negative — can only be in duration. We we *are* is *intemporality.*

## Our Relation To Time

Consciousness cannot be conceptualized without splitting the wholeness or unicity into duality. Duality is then designated by a variety of interdependent counterparts. There are, for instance, the traditional religious terms like heaven and earth, and the more modern and philosophical terms like noumenon and phenomena. A pair of metaphysical terms — intemporality and temporality — would be perhaps most accurate and appropriate. What-We-Are is intemporal; what-we-think-we-are (what we appear to be), that with which we unfortunately identify ourselves, is temporal. In our phenomenal objective aspect, what-we-think-we-are is "time" while in our subjective aspect (as Conciousness) we are "timeless".

Phenomenally, we are "time" because what-we-think-we-are (the psychosomatic apparatus) is something in action. What is in action is in duration, whether the "doing" is physical or psychic, action or thought. An apparent volitional act and the relative volitional reaction, both constitute the infamous *karma*. Obviously, each such apparent action contributes to the composite structure of events which denotes our life in the phenomenal world. The point to note is that this movement in duration does not in any way make us entities separate from some "thing" called "time". All it means is that we are what time Is!

Whether envisaged as a straight line or a curve, "time" has often been compared to a river. Indeed, the simile is almost intuitive and instinctive. It does not need any special kind of wisdom to understand that, since we perceive this river of time as flowing, we must necessarily be outside "time". If we were in the river, we could not be aware of the flow. *Since we perceive the flow of time, we are obviously experiencing it from "outside time", which can only denote intemporality.* What flows in the stream of life, things phenomenal and perceived by our senses (including our bodies), can only be temporal. What-We-Are must necessarily be intemporal, immutable.

It should thus be clear that "time" and "phenomena" are conceptual objectivizations. Also included is our own appearance, with which we are erroneously identified. So, *as phenomena* we are "time" — flowing from waking state to sleeping state, from birth to death, from presence to absence, from appearance to disappearance, from apparent integration to apparent disintegration like any "thing". Time and its interdependent counterpart of intemporality, are separate or polarized opposites only when they are so phenomenally conceived. Noumenally, in their mutual negation in non-phenomenality, they remain inseparably united. In whole mind, when the split mind of phenomenal conceptualization is absent, they are reintegrated as wholeness, neither temporality nor intemporality.

It is for this reason that, intemporally, What-We-Are can be described as "I-Am-Now, Here". "Now" is the vertical, eternal, present moment ("time" being the horizontal flow). "Here" is the eternal infinity (not the temporal "there"). It is in this sense that the Masters' constant advice is: "Just Be."

# The Cosmos And I

We are the sentient beings in the world, and What-We-Are is "I". The cosmos has no nature other than What-We-Are. This is the basic, simple fact of the matter.

There is nothing religious or sanctified about What-We-Are. As sentient objects, we are still objects, though with sentience. All objects are composed of the three dimensions of measurement, plus duration (by means of which they are perceptible in their form). *The measurements, which constitute form, are also its perceiving.* Thus the perceiving becomes identical with that which is perceived. The result is that apart from perceiving itself there remains no room for a perceiver. The forms perceive one another and the perceived form is itself perceiver, perceiving and perceived.

It is important to understand that things become apparent. They do not exist as "things" and their perceiver is all that they are. Again there is thus no room for a projector of form because the imagined projector is the perceiver and there is nothing to be projected. The only "event" is a perceiving of form, and such perceiving is the absolute totality of the event — its origin, its constitution, its appearance. The perceived is its perceiving. In other words, the supposed "event" is just its perceiving, which is its manifestation in its dimensional composition. What this simply means is that *there is no place either for subject or for object. There is only a sensorial perceiving which is an aspect of the noumenality that is all that it is.*

What we are is not separate from what we perceive. Objects are not separate from subject. Phenomena are not separate from noumenon. Nothing phenomenal is separate from what noumenally we *are* and that is utterly formless. As space-time figments we are infinity and intemporality. As concepts we are non-conceptuality.

Materials, characteristics, the "performance" of a "form", are all nothing but interpretive concepts in duration, based on memory (which could be interpreted as "habit-energy"). They are merely details of psychic elaborations that complete the phenomenal picture without adding any pertinent requirement. Similarly, all affective and intellectual manifestations (including the attribution by simple-minded pious people of concepts and emotions to a divinity) are also interpretive psychic elaborations, whose phenomenal *expression* cannot ever be directly noumenal in origin.

Finally, conceptual negation can never be conceived. How can conceiving conceive that which is itself conceiving?! It is what we *are*, neither any-thing nor no-thing. It is just "I", not even I-ness. We, as "I", are this infinite intemporality — "I Am (This) That I Am".

The final Truth is truly simple and obvious — "just in front of your eyes", as the Masters have said. It is precisely like the spectacles through which one looks without seeing them. The point is that "It" cannot be objectivized. Therefore what is needed for an "awakening" is a subjective displacement in order to Be It.

# The Light Of My Eye

The light of my eye is "I"— the vocable "I" expressing itself through manifold manifestations, innumerable "me's" appearing and disappearing every moment.

There is nothing in the Cosmos which light has not found except darkness. When light seeks out darkness, what it finds is the absence of light. The only finding is the understanding that what has been found was the absence of that which was seeking. Asking "who am I" is the light seeking the darkness of a "me", but finding that there is no "who", it can only find a "what" — the absence of the presence of this which is asking the question and seeking the "who". Switch off the search light focussed on the outside object and you will at once see, not the subject (because it would simultaneously become an object), but the absence of what is looking.

Light shines — or appears to shine — only on meeting objective resistance. Light is present everywhere in space (even though the sky may appear to be dark) but is cognizable as such only when it appears to shine through objective reflection from particles in our conceptual atmosphere (when they are sensorially perceived). Any object seen or an event observed has its existence only because "We" have perceived the object or experienced the event. It exists only because one of our senses has recorded the percept or event and has interpreted it in the duality of subject/object. *The object or event does not have any independent existence other than our perceiving of it.*

It is most important to understand, however, that all this appears to happen to us, and that is all we can know about it. All we can know about it is what "we ourselves" think about it. It has no knowable existence of its own. To think of it as being something particular (irrespective of its being an appearance in our psyche) independent of our cognizing of it, is absurd.

The light of my eye which perceives is "I", because there can be no light other than *our* light. Since whatever we are must necessarily be reduced to the vocable "I" (whoever says it, and "anyone" may say it), "I" must be light. " I", as light, manifest only when "I" encounter the apparent resistance of phenomenal objectivity, and thereby "I" shine because shining is the apparent nature (*dharma*) of light. When all apparent objects are removed — when consciousness ceases to function in deep sleep or under sedation — all objects and "I" remain in the potentiality of the static aspect of consciousness. This is the not-shining of light or the apparent darkness of space. It is consciousness in the absence of movement, in the absence of resistance.

It is What-I-Am that does the seeing. It is the luminosity of the totality of functioning — the vocable "I" — which produces the appearance of action and renders all action universal. The supposed individuals concerned in all apparent action are merely phenomenal *reflections* like any other objects, and nothing more, like the reflections of the moon in pools of water.

## Liberation From Self

I may believe that the whole universe is a dream and that all the human beings and the other sentient beings are dreamed characters within that dream, but so long as the I is a self who considers himself as being outside that dream, I must necessarily be no nearer to the awakening from that dream. This is so because liberation is nothing other than liberation from this idea of a self or "me". *It is only when the "me" is included in the visionary universe, and the apperception does not include a "me" to apperceive as the apperceiver,* that the "I" can occupy the position vacated by the "me". Then the apperception comports the realization that the seeker and the sought is the same.

The "self" as a phenomenon is merely an appearance like all phenomena, and therefore devoid of autonomous and independent nature, just as a shadow cannot have any such nature. As an entity, "self" is only an erroneous concept. In other words, "I" is totally absent in mere appearance, and "I" cannot be an object at all. Liberation from bondage is nothing other than being completely permeated by this understanding, and there cannot be liberation without the total annihilation of the notion of phenomenal identity as "self" or "me".

The simple truth is that no "me" can be liberated because there is no objective "me" that is in bondage. Simply, there is no "me" at all! Freedom can only be freedom from one's idea of oneself. The notion of one's "self" is one's only bondage. Indeed, *any effort by a "self" to liberate "itself" would merely mean steadily strengthening the very obstacle* it is seeking to remove.

What is necessary is the abolition of the notion of a "self", the dis-appearance of the conceptual appearance which, one knows, is not what one *is*. For this to happen, the way cannot possibly be either meditation (sitting thinking) or premeditation (sitting thinking of not-thinking) or unpremeditation (sitting not-thinking about not-thinking). All these methods or processes must necessarily involve a "me" who is meditating or premeditating or unpremeditating, towards an end which seeks to abolish the notion of the very "me" who is doing it.  Such processes or methods may indeed produce certain results (which may or may not be harmful) but never the one result that matters, the one that is sought.  The answer lies only in a spontaneous "letting-go" of all desire and effort, a true surrender, which is itself only the result of a deep understanding!

# The Child Of A Barren Woman

The questions, whether someone is ignorant or enlightened and whether someone is subject to destiny or free-will, are both utterly misconceived. Neither is a question at all, because the premises on which the questions are based are false. There just is no entity to be called "someone" to which either condition would be relevant, either physically or metaphysically.

The fact of the matter is that the "someone" is merely a psyche-soma (a body-mind) that is quite incapable of exercising any kind of independence or autonomy. The psyche-soma is merely an appearance. It is merely a vision that is subject to one of the two ways in which the mechanism of phenomenality could be envisaged. Whether the process of manifestation is explained by a principle based on the notion of causality, or by one that is based on statistical probability, it really makes no difference. Whatever the principle ("law") that is used to explain the mechanism of manifestation, the point is that all such laws are merely schematic conceptual structures. Moreover, all the "someones" are merely appearances within the totality of manifestation and not separate entities. No form of objectivization could possibly have any nature of its own. Even physicists now accept that the "observer" is himself a "factor" in the experiment.

If the nature of a "someone" as a psyche-soma is clearly understood, then all problems will be at once be seen to be problems concerning the "child of a barren woman", as Nisargadatta Maharaj used to say. Whatever thinks it is in bondage or is free, that which thinks it is determined or is exercising volition (free-will), is identified in thought with a phenomenal object and *appears* to be subject to the particular condition. That is to say, the "someone" who thinks he is free, whether as being enlightened or as having free-will, is as much in "bondage" as the "someone" who thinks he is bound.

The supposed problem of the supposed phenomenal entity disappears entirely if it is seen that the noumenal aspect of any "one" is precisely the same as that of any other phenomenon. That is to say, "one" is noumenality itself. Any problem is only apparent because the seeker of the solution to the problem — whether it concerns bondage and liberation, or, free-will and destiny — is still an apparent identity and no identity can ever find its own absence. Hence, the oft-asked question by Nisargadatta Maharaj: "Who wants to know?"!

A self-anchored phenomenon, that which thinks it is in bondage or free, determined or exercising free-will, is identified in thought (in conceptualizing) with a phenomenal object. It *appears* subject to that condition to which such thought is attached. A self-anchored phenomenon cannot find the noumenon (that it really is) any more than a shadow can find its substance. Most importantly therefore, the exercise of volition by way of any kind of practice must necessarily be futile and defeat its own purpose.

## Nobody Believes That He Does Not Exist

When the disciple goes to the *guru* wanting to know his real nature, the *guru* tells him that the only thing he needs to know is that he does not exist as an entity. His astonishment turns into perplexity when he sees that the *guru* is not making a joke but is intensely serious. It is perhaps much later that he would understand that nobody has ever believed that he does not exist. This is because there is no entity to believe that he does not exist. If there were an entity, such an entity, in maintaining that it did not exist, would automatically thereby prove its existence.

What is present cannot say that it is absent. This is of course a truism. What is the point in stressing it? The point — perhaps the most important and basic point — is that the one who is seeking the answer is the absence of that which he is not. This means that there can be a "you" only so long as there is thinking by a phenomenal object, an objective appearance, a "you" that thinks it is bound and seeks liberation. As soon as the thinking-process ceases (as in deep sleep or under sedation), there is no "you" either considering that it is bound or seeking any liberation This makes it clear that the "you" is purely an inferential entity who assumes that he is bound. In other words, the "me" concept has no permanence as such, and its absences are as inevitable as its presences, both being recurrent and intermittent. But while the presences are totally in temporality, the absences are intemporal. This is because while presence in duration means absence intemporally, temporal absence (being absence of presence) is also intemporal absence.

To put the matter differently, and perhaps more accurately, absence of identification with the "me" concept means the absence of a presence in duration, and therefore comports its intemporal absence also. It is thus totally outside the sphere of space-time continuum, before time ever was. It is therefore eternal.

To put it in yet another way, when subject is looking outside, subject sees object. When subject itself is seen looking at its object, subject becomes object and is no longer subject. This is like the cameraman snapped in the act of snapping his object. When subject turns round and looks within at itself, what it sees is *not* subject (because then it would still be looking at an object) but "nothing" at all because subject, *as such*, cannot be seen. Only objects can be seen. Subject as such is the absence of anything seen or seeable. This is the "mirror-void", which reveals everything but retains nothing. This is the absence of identification with a "me" concept. This is the transcendence of subject-object relationship. This is the total absence which is the presence of all that appears to be. This is the total absence from which arises the concepts of presence of presence and presence of absence.

# The Basic Logic Of The Void

So long as we are employing thought there is conceptualizing and our mind is split, and every concept is subject to interdependent opposites or counterparts. The question of dual counterparts, of a perpetual regression (God created the world, but who created God, and so on) can cease only when the whole-mind is involved. Thus, as soon as it is apperceived that total phenomenal absence means total noumenal presence, there is no more objectivizing through dual concepts. As soon as it is understood that *total phenomenal absence is the same as total noumenal presence* (that they are one, and never can they be two), there cannot be any beyond. Apperceiving means the transcending of the process of objectivizing and the return of functioning to the source, with the whole mind functioning directly.

The phenomenal (appearance or form), and its interdependent opposite the non-phenomenal (non-appearance or formlessness), are both conceptual. The source of the phenomenal and the non-phenomenal is "noumenon", which is not the interdependent counterpart of "phenomenon". Noumenon is a symbol indicating double phenomenal absence inasmuch as it is the absence of both counterparts (phenomenal and non-phenomenal). Even so, all this is conceptual, and thus "noumenon" becomes an objective concept requiring a "cognizer" of something cognized.

The noumenon is conceived as non-being, a shapeless emptiness, the potential "void" out of which the myriad things are engendered. So the non-being or "void" in fact amounts to an attempt to objectify subjectivity. This fact must be very clearly seen and understood because otherwise one would forever be tempted to conceive it *objectively* whether as "inconceivable" nothingness (void), or as the mysterious source of all things. The very fact of trying to conceive it as an object — "inconceivable" though it is imagined — implies hanging on to the habitual way of seeking to objectify every perception.

And the heart of the matter is that unless this habit of turning every percept into an objective concept is abandoned, the essential understanding cannot ever begin to develop.

Whatever is conceived as the "void" or nothingness cannot be an object at all. It is what the perceiver of it is. It cannot be seen either to exist or not to exist, for it cannot be seen at all!

What really happens is that the perceiver at this juncture is trying to look at what he is after having reached a sort of dead-end. What should really happen now is that the perceiver should turn right round and wake up to the truth that he is face to face with his own nature. The void of the dead-end is precisely what the eye sees when it attempts to look at itself. Enlightenment happens when it is apperceived that the notions of "non-existence" or "void" or "emptiness" are indeed futile and empty. Such notions are merely the indications or pointers that the end of the intellectual road has been reached. Apperception happens the moment the seeker turns round and finds that he is already at the destination. He is home. The seeker is himself what he has been seeking!

Saint Jnaneshwar, in his *Amritanubhava*\*, says that he got rid of the conceptual cognizer of the difference between the voidness of nullity and the voidness of the potential plenum by the grace of his *guru*—by surrendering his conceptual individuality at the feet of his *guru* and thereby annihilating it.

---

\*     See the authors translation w/commentary of this work:
*Experience Of Immortality* (Bombay: Chetana, 1984)

# The Substantial "I" And The Shadowy "me"

"I" (Consciousness) can never be conscious of anything. Why? Because Consciousness is all that I Am. A separate entity, individual, self, ego or "me" concept is an object. "I" become an object as soon as I think of myself. Whenever I act as myself, it is an object that acts. However, on these rare occasions when I act directly, spontaneously, then no I acts. Why? Because "I" am the source of all thought and of all doing, not the thinker of the thought, nor the performer of any act.

What does this mean? This means that there is no cognizer independent of the object cognized, nor any object cognized independently of the cognizer of it. *The "cognizer" and the "cognized" are not two but are merely the counterparts of the act of cognition.* Together they constitute the function of cognizing, the functional aspect of noumenality or pure potentiality which as such cannot have any phenomenal existence other than its manifestation as the interrelated objects, cognizer and cognized. The observer cannot observe the observer. The eye cannot see the eye that sees.

Where does this lead us? This leads us to realize the absurdity of phenomenal objects desperately seeking for themselves as subject. How could an object possibly seek and find its subject? All that an object thinks it is doing is done by the subject, all it *is* is subject. Therefore the seeking means the subject itself is desperately seeking for itself! The shadow is nothing other than the substance. How can the shadow eliminate itself? Indeed, there is no "thing" to aim at, or hunt, or look for. On ceasing to seek, one is present as Presence, noumenal presence or phenomenal absence. The positive act of searching is inevitably that which, by externalizing itself, turns itself away from what it is.

This, of which one is conscious, is an object, a thing. Everything is "I", and I am no thing. What I am objectively, is the *totality* of phenomenal manifestation, the objectivization of subjectivity. What-I-Am subjectively is what all phenomena are. Is there anything inherently personal about it at any stage? Never. Indeed, the intrusion of the personal element is the whole trouble, the infamous "bondage".

It is only when we know that we are not the inferential phenomenal object that we think we are, that the immense potentiality that is our noumenal non-being will be realized.

Non-being? Of course, because "being" is "becoming" since it has within itself the impregnated notion of duration.

# BOOK THREE

*The Individual And His Problem*

# The Individual And Nature (Nisarga)

From the earliest possible age, an infant is conditioned to regard nature not as something of which he is an integral part (which his deepest instinct tells him he is) but as something alien, something to be conquered and exploited for his individual needs. This broad view (and purpose) gets suitably amended according to the changing scientific vogues and intellectual fashions. But the underlying estrangement has continued unabated. The view prevails that the needs of man require that man himself should actively take over the management of the world, including its ecology. The lazy way in which the evolution of life and nature has taken place over the last several million years can no longer be allowed. Difficult though the task may be, nature and life must be *controlled* by the individual man, and not be allowed to take its normal natural course. The few, comparatively paltry, achievements of science have blinded man to the inescapable fact that the subtle balance and harmony in the universe has been maintained through extraordinarily complex processes of nature. Of these processes, man has but the haziest comprehension.

This situation has certain interesting aspects. When Konrad Zuse developed one of the first functioning computers, he foresaw the computer as helping man to unravel the deepest secrets of nature. And so it has. In theoretical physics it is hardly feasible to conduct significant experiments without using computers. In telecommunications, and even in the private sphere, the computer is clearly leading to important changes. It is quite clear that technological development in general is bound to be greatly accelerated in the near future. Computers are becoming more compact and better equipped with larger storage capacity. And the interesting aspect of the matter is that it is more than likely that in the next century, certain types of factories will be developed by computers working on their own, at first partially and then totally. Already, today, computers are involved to a large extent in the design of computer components, and are able to direct the subsequent manufacturing process almost without human intervention. This advance could possibly make the working individual completely out of date. It is expected that systems will be created that will reproduce themselves. Could the state of things reach a stage where the computer would *think* that nature — *including the human being* — is a world to be conquered and controlled by technology and not something to be allowed to just happen? Could the computer in course of time take over from the human intellect which today forgets that its roots are in the very organism it now presumes to improve? The fact of the matter is that the technical rational consciousness is as alien to the natural man as was the supernatural soul. Both nature and the natural man are viewed as objects. They are studied always by a technique which makes them external and therefore different from the subjective observer. In other words, our ideas of what nature is like *on the inside*, are merely concepts from outside, mere guesses at the mercy of educated fashion. Knowledge of nature from the inside can *happen* only through natural, spontaneous intuition. This is due to a split, a schism between body and mind, spirit and nature, subject and object, controller and controlled, the polaric opposites.

Greater *scientific* knowledge, however, has made the individual human realize that all these divisions are actually misleading terms. They refer to a world wherein all events are clearly interdependent: "an immense complexity of subtly balanced relationships which, like an endless knot, has no loose end from which it can be untangled and put in supposed order". This means in effect that in this world of interdependent polaric relationships (a seamless unity) *nothing can have any meaningful existence except in terms of something else.* Therefore, it is quite ridiculous for man to consider this world as something outside of himself, as something he can control from without, with his roots established outside the world which he is considering. Man and nature are one phenomenon, not two. Just as, indeed, the phenomenon and the noumenon (whether considered in terms of non-phenomenon or in terms of that which is prior to both) are one, not two. All there is, is Consciousness, whether it is at rest as the subjective unmanifest or it is in movement as the objective manifest. As Nisargadatta Maharaj used to point out repeatedly, a deep understanding, an apperception of this unity, is Truth, Enlightenment, God, or whatever.

The fact of the matter is that the individual human, unaware of this unity, pulls in one direction and finds himself in turn pulled in the opposite direction. He does not know the origin of the thought which makes him pull in a particular direction. He considers himself separate from his environment. He does not truly know whether any action of his is really of his own volition or is predetermined. He thinks he can shape his own destiny and yet is piteously anxious to know his future from a seer or an astrologer. He does not realize that his confusion lies within and not without. It lies in the tangle of his conceptualization and not in the convolutions of the endless knot

In spite of the pronouncements of the modern scientist confirming the interconnectedness of all things and events, and the basic oneness of all phenomena, (including the individual human), man's total involvement with nature is still viewed with considerable suspicion and concern. This is because the individual human just cannot accept the fact that his individuality, and more importantly his individual volition, is no more than an illusion. Even more significant is the frightening realization that man's oneness with nature in a seamless unity ineluctably implies that the individual's impulses, urges and ideals, his very motivations, are in fact, nothing more than "abstract intellectual ghosts". And therefore the individual's life, as an integral part of the universal life of events, can have no individual purpose or special meaning. This thought frightens the individual because without his ideals and motivations, he is a "nothing" in the nothingness of a purposeless world.

In actuality, purpose (ideals) as the basis of an individual's life is nothing but conditioning. The loss of this apparent basis is frightening only because the focus of interest has mistakenly shifted from the event itself to its reaction on the ego from the viewpoint of the illusory purposes and ideals. The meaning and purpose behind acts and events have significance only for human beings, not for the other sentient beings. Only the individual human considers time or duration as an independent phenomenon which affects him. Thus, to consider that the world has no meaning or purpose is to say that the world is not centered on humanity. As the *Tao Te Ching* puts it, "Heaven and Earth are not human-hearted." What is not human in nature seems inhuman only when the matter is considered from the viewpoint of the separated individual human, who sees it as a separate part of the totality. The question is never asked: if nature is not human in certain of its aspects and has no purpose as envisaged by the individual human, then what does it have in place of the purpose which it does not have? Nature is not to be seen in terms of human thought, logic and language. These are necessary only for man who is in an entirely different context. The *rest* of nature is not concerned with the language and logic of man. As some writer has put it, "may it not be that when we speak of nature as blind, and of matter-energy as unintelligent, we are simply projecting upon them the blankness which we feel when we try to know our own consciousness as an object, when we try to see our eyes (without the help of a mirror) or taste our own tongues?"

The fact of the matter is that the individual human considers himself superior to the other sentient beings because he is endowed with intellect which leads to the acquisition of rational thought and conscious attention. He forgets, however, that the individual human organism is not basically different from an inanimate object. It has the same integration, at the moment of its "birth" or "appearance", as an inanimate object. Its cells do disintegrate or die, but they continually reintegrate into the same individual pattern of concentrated energy (body). In other words, whilst the inanimate object is only born once and only dies once, the living organism is born, dies and is reborn ceaselessly until it finally disintegrates at the end of this period of its "life". The human organism, *in addition* to the two essences of the inanimate and animate phenomenal objects, is endowed with the third essence of "intellect". It is this third essence — the intellect — which makes the individual human think that he is a separate entity with autonomy and independence of choice and action concerning his individual aims and ideals. In other words, the individual human is "made" of the same basic elements *plus* sentience *plus* intellect, and is an intrinsic part of the totality of nature. If, therefore, the individual human thinks (because of his intellectual processes) that he has his own aims and purposes and ideals in what he considers his "life", the totality of nature is quite unconcerned about them. The inanimate, the animate and the human are all manifestations, (on three different planes) of the same Consciousness, the same cosmic mind-energy.

It is only because we have lost the sense or the feeling of the wholeness of the endless knot, that we think of action in terms of the alternatives of freedom and fate, voluntarism and determinism. We forget that these terms are truly interconnected and polaric. The real problem is not that we have developed the sense of individual or personalized consciousness but that we consider this to be incompatible with the feeling of expanded consciousness which would enable us to see and feel nature from within. The fact of the matter is that the two are not only not incompatible, but that our individual perception is indeed all the better, all the keener, against the background of totality. Then our perception has perspective. The individual leaf can be seen in its full clarity not in separation but only in relation to the branch and the tree. We can truly appreciate an individual figure in a painting only in relation to, and against the background of, the whole painting.

To see and feel nature from within means *not* asking *what* the world is. The "what" implies classification and measurement. Classification is a human achievement which separates the human from nature, and separation means conflict and unhappiness. Separation means a boundary line, and a boundary line means a battle line To ask what something is in its natural state is a misconception. To ask what a rose is, is to miss the point altogether because the rose cannot be anything other than our experience of it. The only way to find out what anything is in its natural state is to perceive it with a silent mind, to *be* that. The warmness or coolness of water can only be experienced, it cannot be described. This silent perceiving or cognizing is precisely what is meant by "feel", as such, not the personal feeling.

Excessive verbal communication has become so compulsive and widespread that it is taken for granted as the only way to understand anything. There is the incident of the Japanese artist Hasagawa bursting out in exasperation at his western students with their ceaseless request for explanations with the remark: "What is the matter with you? Aren't you able *to feel?*" It can be understood from this why there is so much myth in almost every religion. The myth is the easiest way to make the simple and unlearned listener get the "feel" of what is being said at the metaphysical level. This is what is generally ignored or forgotten when the sophisticated scholar analyzes, criticizes and belittles the myths in the organized religions.

The naturalism of the *Tao*, the Chinese system of practical philosophy, is essentially a way of life in which the individual or personal consciousness is in operation while retaining the original feeling of the seamless unity of nature. What it involves is a completely new way of thinking and acting. It addresses the function of effort, discipline and exercise of will power, as well as the pursuit of pleasure. It is based on the understanding that any action considered as a result of personal effort means strengthening the ego and the divided mind. Indeed, even deliberate "positive" actions resulting from this supposed understanding are not natural. Such actions are themselves the result of *a false understanding by the ego*. And it is because of this very fact that Nisargadatta Maharaj repeatedly asseverated that the natural act is that in which the ego is not present. The natural act can only be the spontaneously emanating effect of the right understanding itself. It contains no positive personal effort.

The essence of apperception, which leads to natural action, is a deep understanding which accepts all psychosomatic organisms as vehicles or instruments through which the totality of Nature functions. Each action, each event, becomes spontaneity which is the essence of all natural action. It is the "controlled accident" of being able to do precisely the right thing at the right time, at the right place, without any self-conscious volition or purpose. The depth of such understanding comports the realization that all events, though perhaps not very acceptable in the immediate context, are indeed part of the totality. There is truly no individual who can be seen as the perpetrator of events and therefore there can be no "enemy". The result is that it becomes a habit to take life as it comes. Events are witnessed as they occur, without reading into them any individual as the cause, or any pattern in the events which affects one individually. The focus of interest remains neither the past nor the future but the *present moment*, "the still point of the turning world" and "the center of the rotation of seasons."

It is necessary to realize that the true return to natural spontaneity neither demands any break in what-is nor any change, such as back-to-nature romanticism. This is so because natural spontaneity essentially means the willing acceptance of What-Is in the present moment, without any desire to change it. Any desire and action to change what-is is the misconceived volition of the individual. It cannot possibly be natural spontaneity. The usual question at this stage is: is the individual then to live like a vegetable? The answer is: natural and spontaneous action will follow in the ordinary course, according to the inherent temperament and capacity of each organism, since each is an integral part of nature. It is only when this natural action is interrupted by the working of the split-mind that the harmonious flow of the natural action is broken and conflict results. The split-mind thinks in terms of the acceptable and the unacceptable as irreconcilable opposites, without really knowing what is truly acceptable and what is not. What seems acceptable today in certain circumstances, may not seem so tomorrow in other circumstances. What the split-mind does is analogous to a dancer interrupting his dance with a simultaneous effort to understand and explain to himself the precise significance of each movement. Such an effort must necessarily be a disaster.

What then is the individual supposed to do? Very simply, to remember that he is an individual trying to swim against the current; and to realize that there truly is nothing for the separate illusory individual (he is in every way an integral part of the totality of Nature) to do. He need only float with the magnificent current of totality in the ecstasy (not frustration) of his oneness with the cosmic current. What does the dreamer do with his dream, except passively witness it without judgement? What can a spectator do except to witness any spectacle over which he has no control? What can anyone do in any situation over which he has absolutely no control? Just let go! Because the situation truly is not outside him. He is the situation. And the piquant point is that there is truly no individual to deliberately and consciously "let go"! When there is apperception, when the understanding becomes an unshakable conviction, the letting-go happens on its own. Then there is no individual who is expected to let go. In other words, the true understanding comports the conviction that the "individual" is a mental image, an illusion which itself was an obstruction to the letting-go.

What is the basis of this apperception which brings about the understanding and the consequent letting-go? It is an *intensity* of feeling, the faith that all feelings have an inherent ambivalence. It is *knowing* that there is an inescapable polarity of elation and depression, love and hate, humility and pride. Therefore, nature itself must contain this ambivalence without which perpetual joy would be as meaningless as a meal restricted to only sweet things. "Good" would have no meaning without "evil".

Excessive verbal expression becomes a drag on genuine feelings. It is undoubtedly for this reason that in *Advaita* in India, *Zen* in Japan and *Tao* in China, the real center is not the creative inventions of ideas but an ineffable *experience* that is concrete and non-verbal. Thus the spirit, as distinguished from phenomenal nature, the *dharma* (suchness) of various things, is not seen in such sharp contrast in the Eastern traditions. Spirit is *not* considered as a separation from nature (such as the abstract from the concrete), but as the direct experience of the totality of nature in its non-conceptual state.

Verbal communication, "the characteristic disease of the West", is seen in its naked form in the question "What is it?" that generally precedes every form of manifestation. There cannot possibly be any description to explain *what* the natural world is. The question itself is an indication of the extent and the depth of the verbal conditioning that has taken place. What the question clearly implies is "how do you *classify* it?" All classification is a human invention, and the natural state does not emanate with any given classification. Words can separate what appears naturally as inseparable, but *words cannot actually separate what is intrinsically inseparable*. The only way to keep separation away is to keep words, that is, thoughts, away from the feeling, *so that what is natural may be felt in the silent mind*. And, when thought is spent, when conceptualization is absent, the individual is no longer a separate entity. It gets merged in the silent Consciousness as its intrinsic essence. Such silent perception is the "feel" which brings about the recovery of what was once the infant's inherent sense of integrity with the natural world.

Conceptualization sees nature — and life — as something constructed or built upon a certain set of principles or laws, like the plan of a building. Indeed, conceptualization sees "God" as the maker of a world with a certain purpose and meaning which the individual, as a separate entity, is expected to discover for himself. The Eastern mysticism — *Advaita* in India, *Tao* in China, and *Zen* in Japan — on the other hand, sees phenomenal nature not as a deliberate creation, but as a spontaneous emanation or arising, organic rather than mechanical. Understanding nature thus, becomes not an intellectual exercise, but a direct experience in mental silence. It is most important to understand very clearly that this state of mental silence does not mean keeping the mind dull or empty. Indeed, thought itself is very much a part of the natural functioning of Totality and is therefore not an "outsider". The point is that *wordless contemplation can exist coincidentally with thinking* when such thinking is witnessed without judgement and, therefore, without involvement. What transpires then is an absence of the mind ceaselessly trying to split itself by *simultaneously* trying to act and judge, to think and reflect on such thinking. There is an absence of "mental mitosis". There is an absence of a vicious circle of thoughts about thoughts about thoughts. It is like *not* struggling in a whirlpool. This means in effect "non-striving" against a current, or floating at ease.

The first experience of seeing a photographic image being developed — the emerging of the whole image on the paper or the film — is very often a startling experience because one is so conditioned to think of a thing as being constructed piece by piece. Similarly, to watch the formation of a crystal is a fascinating experience: it appears in the solution altogether at once and not piece by piece. Perhaps the fascination is an expression of the intuitive feeling we have that the phenomenal universe is a spontaneous, whole concurrent occurrence. It also seems to stun one's intellect to see the lines of forces in a magnetic field constellating themselves in iron filings in a sudden rush and not appearing serially. Perhaps because it is such a common sight, one does not realize it, but an infant grows, not bit by bit, but with its *whole form* growing from within, like a plant stem. This "within", growing spontaneously, is what nature is. It is quite unlike a God who is supposed to have created the world from "outside". Once this within-ness is realized, all sense of separation gets wondrously healed and the interconnectedness of things-events and the oneness of the universe is *felt* without the need of intellectual analysis.

The truly within cannot be an object because it is prior to the conceptualized triad of observ*er* — observ*ed* — observ*ing*. What we really are is this inwardness or withinness which expresses itself in the formation and working of our complex nervous systems. The individual contents himself with focusing his attention on (identifying himself with) the narrow, superficial area of the conscious and the voluntary. He forgets or ignores the truly vital unconscious and the involuntary. The idea of the separate "me" is so firmly established in our psyches that our very breath and the beat of our hearts appear to belong to something other than the "me". It is thus convenient to think of God as a superhuman entity in comparison with the puny "me", to think in terms of a God who has created the world and is in charge of its working, including all the unconscious processes in the body. God is thus conceived as being simply "a colossal magnification and multiplication of the conscious, analytical mode of knowledge". It is a marvelous conception which has at its root the monstrosity of a decapitated consciousness without any inwardness, knowing everything including Himself, thoroughly transparent to His own *conscious* understanding. *His subjectivity is thus made completely objective!*

If we analyze this concept, we find that at its root lies the old problem of seeing pairs of opposites as wholly unrelated instead of seeing them as interrelated polar opposites, the very warp and woof of phenomenal nature. The individual in associating death and decay with evil, conceives God as "being" and "life", as opposed to "non-being" and "death". This totally ignores the basic fact that pure being and pure non-being are both conceptual myths. But as soon as the inner identity of these inseparable correlatives is felt with total conviction, so is the identity between the individual and nature. Then death is accepted as part of living, a return to that unknown inwardness out of which the individual was born as an intrinsic part of nature.

# The Individual And The Opposites In Life

One of the biggest mysteries of nature, and perhaps the basis of man's unhappiness, is the existence of opposites. Not irreversible, irreconcilable opposites, but interrelated, polaric opposites. The kind in which one cannot exist without the other and, indeed, one is the very reason for the existence of the other. Polarity is something significantly more than mere opposition or duality. It means that the opposites are joined together *inseparably*, like the two ends of a stick or the two faces of a coin or the two poles of a magnet. What is called a magnet and has the properties of a magnet would not be a magnet but for the two opposite poles.

The polaric opposites become the basis of man's unhappiness because in considering the opposites in life, the human individual forgets that the poles themselves are nothing more than mere abstract "terms" or "symbols". He forgets that what is really significant and important is not terms or symbols but what lies between the two poles. This is the problem of the individual's unhappiness because thinking in symbols means separating experiences into various classes and notional "intellectual pigeonholes". In other words, the human individual thinks in terms of individuality, and thus manages to divide in conceptualization what is truly undivided in nature. Is it surprising that this unnatural dichotomy should separate the human being from his natural background and put him in a state of mind that he calls "unhappiness" or "misery" or "bondage"? And finding himself in this state is it surprising that he is forever seeking liberation?

Nature itself does not seem to know — or care — about the man-made opposites or about this world of opposites. Nature seems perfectly satisfied and happy to produce a world of infinite, rapturous variety that knows nothing about anything pretty or ugly, ethical or unethical. As Thoreau has said, nature never apologizes, never sees the need of it, obviously because it sees only delightful variety, not "errors of opposites". It is worth noting that it is the basic polarity of nature itself, on which the ancient Chinese culture has been founded.

This is what Lao Tzu has said on this most important matter:

*When everyone recognizes beauty as beautiful*
*there is already ugliness;*
*When everyone recognizes goodness as good,*
*there is already evil.*
*"To be" and "not to be" arise mutually;*
*Difficult and easy are mutually realized;*
*Long and short are mutually contrasted;*
*High and low are mutually posited;*
*Before and after are in mutual sequence.*

And Chuang Tzu, Lao Tzu's illustrious successor has said:

"Thus, those who say that they would have right without its correlate, wrong, good government without its correlate, misrule, do not apprehend the great principles of the universe, nor the nature of all creation. One might as well talk of the existence of Heaven without that of the Earth, or of the negative principle without the positive which is clearly impossible. Yet people keep on discussing it without stop; such people must be either fools or knaves."

Many people, especially Westerners, would firmly accept as the perfect philosopher, Aristotle, who considers that all action is choice and that the will moves into action only in so far as to make a choice, wise or otherwise, good in preference to something evil. Not so acceptable would be Heraclitus who holds that "it is one and the same thing to be living or dead, awake or asleep, young or old". By and large, as one modern philosopher has put it, Western culture is a celebration of the illusion that good may exist without evil, light without darkness, and pleasure without pain. The *modern* Eastern culture is not lagging far behind this view. Ironically though, the modern Western culture — and the modern physics — find a strong attraction towards the ancient Eastern wisdom.

Modern physics has now left no room to doubt the essential polaric relationship in all nature. The age-old monumental separation of mass from energy has fallen to the Einsteinian equation. The fact that the two ancient opposites of mass and energy are just two aspects of one phenomenon has been all too horrendously demonstrated in Hiroshima. Rest and motion have become quite indistinguishable — "each is both" — because what one observer sees as an object at rest, another observer, *at the same time*, sees as being in motion. Quantum mechanics has turned the previously accepted "laws" of nature upside down and rendered them totally obsolete. The dichotomy between particle and wave has vanished. The "wavicle" has emerged, and the split between structure and function has evaporated. What is more, the new laws of physics have demolished the separation between the observer and the observed object to the extent that the observer is now an active "participant" in the spectacle his senses pick up. There is more than a mild suggestion that the dynamics of the observer's consciousness may not be separable from the dynamics of the world. What this means, in other words, is that there truly is neither an observer nor an observed object but simply and precisely, the function of observ-*ing*.

It is not that opposites are not seen in life, but rather that underneath these opposites (which are necessarily interrelated) there is a basic unity. It is because of this situation that time and space, subject and object, are now treated by science for all practical purposes as being so intricately interdependent that they form a single unified organic pattern. What is now given due importance is not the opposing phenomena, but the event which they both together bring about.

An object needs space to appear in its three dimensions, but it can never be perceived unless there is duration or time in which the perceiving can take place. Therefore space and time cannot truly be understood separately, except notionally for a specific analysis. And even such analysis would miss its true significance unless space-time is seen as one concept. In other words, from the viewpoint of "the coincidence of opposites" (what Nicholas of Cusa called the *coincidential oppositorum*), what were generally considered as entirely irreconcilable opposites have turned out to be complementary aspects of one and the same phenomenon.

It is on these considerations that Alfred North Whitehead's philosophy of "organism" and "vibratory existence" is based. It proposes that all the basic elements are in their essence "vibratory". This is what Nisargadatta Maharaj also repeatedly asserted. He went so far as to say that all things and events, both welcomed and dreaded by human beings, are the results of these vibrations of the elements, concordant or conflicting as the case may be. In Whitehead's words, "a vibratory ebb and flow of any underlying energy or activity" is what describes the elements in the universe. What this means is that there cannot be a phenomenon like, say, a wave without the opposing aspects of a high and a low, a crest and a hollow, a high point and a low point.

I remember as a small boy avoiding the specs of dust illumined by a ray of the sun coming in from the window. It was quite a shock to learn later that the sun's ray did not bring the particles of dust, that the dust was present everywhere and that all that the sun's ray did was to bring them into prominence. As the Gestalt theory of perception says, we are not aware of an object or figure or event (any phenomenon), except in relation to a contrasting background. However stark may be the contrast between the star and its background of darkness, the one cannot be perceived in the absence of the other. In other words, an image, a tactile impression or a sound is recognizable only in contrast with relative formlessness or relative silence, and vice versa. It is interesting to note that in experiments concerning "sensory deprivation", where the individual's perception is exposed to nothing but background, he finds it necessary to supply the missing figuration by fantasy. Such "pattern completion" takes place in both seeing and hearing. Localized regions of visual defects and the perceived visual patterns surrounding blind spots (scotomas) are extended through the non-seeing area by the perceiving brain. Similarly, in experiments where a short word in a recorded sentence cannot be heard because of sound disturbance, subjects have still reported hearing the complete sentence.

All this translated into kinesthetics, says Alan Watts, amounts to the understanding that there cannot be any awareness of motion except in relation to stillness, or of the freedom of motion except in relation to a certain amount of resistance. It is revealing that Nisargadatta Maharaj used to say that manifestation cannot occur without a relationship of arrest and movement. He further reiterated that consciousness is essentially a sensation of effort and frustration, and that the first stirring of the consciousness — the thought "I Am" (the big bang of astronomy and physics) — was a tremendous moan into the state of awareness of existence from the absolute still state of unawareness.

The whole point of this exposition is that the misery and unhappiness of the individual human being is due almost entirely to his ignoring this basic fact of unity in the universe. Homer explained in a burst of compassion for the human race, "Would that strife might perish from amongst gods and men." But, says Heraclitus, "Homer was wrong...if that were to occur, then all things would cease to exist."

In the same manner, all our feelings have significance only in relation to their relative opposites. While the human individual abhors pain and discomfort, he would never be able to understand, let alone appreciate, pleasure and comfort by themselves. And yet, in his abysmal ignorance he forgets this basic fact of life and strives with all his might for pleasure without pain, and life without death. What has been said about the interdependence and interrelationship of pleasure and pain (and all the other apparent opposites) is not really difficult for the intellect to understand and accept. And yet, there is something which seems to hold the human individual back from living his life within this seemingly simple understanding. That is that he is so proud of the fact that he can think. He now even considers himself capable, in due course, of creating life itself. And it is precisely because of this boundary that he has created between himself within and the entire world without, that he has forgotten his true nature. He has been asking himself repeatedly in his more "lucid" moments the question "Who am I". And the greatest tragedy is that the question itself is the primary separation! No other animal is concerned with this question. And the joke is that with this question man has put himself in a supposed bondage. It is *the pursuit of this very question* — (not the answer because there truly is none) — that will lead him to the discovery that the human individual is quite illusory and that the individual cannot have any existence as an independent and autonomous entity. His existence in the universe is essentially only as a part of this universe, and this universe is the objective expression of the subjective absolute. It is a universe that is "not composed of dead matter, but is, on the contrary, a living Presence", in which the Absolute is immanent.

It should therefore be clear that man's real and basic problem is that he has himself created the problem. First he separates himself from the rest of the manifestation. Then he wants, as a separate and independent entity, a part of life and not the whole of it. He wants what he considers acceptable and rejects what is not. The individual does not realize that in wanting only the crest of pleasure and not the hollow of pain, he is merely striving after illusions which can lead only to frustration and misery, culminating in the utter terror of physical death. The way the average person "thinks" is by paying attention to one term of a relationship (the positive, or the pleasant, or the figure) and ignoring the other term (the negative, the unpleasant, the ground). The result is that, *without realizing it*, his viewpoint becomes distorted. Thought and its processes get developed to the exclusion of intuition as the infant grows into childhood, and then very soon, the person confidently thinks of himself as an individual figure exclusive of the ground of nature.

There may be wisdom in the saying "Give the Devil his due" because this appreciation of the two hands of God — the good and the bad — is truly what distinguishes the esoteric from the exoteric aspect of religion. The esoteric aspect is present in almost every religion, and certainly in all organized religions, but it is found to be generally guarded and kept closed because of the fact that this mystical aspect of religion is not easily intelligible. The average person is likely to be confused about the underlying unity of the opposites. Any attempt to explain this aspect of religion to those who are not intellectually and spiritually "ready for it" could not only confuse them intellectually but in practice also make ordinary life almost impossible to live. As it is, even those who are naturally attracted to this esoteric aspect — and seem to understand the basis of it — are still baffled when a sage like Nisargadatta Maharaj tells them "understanding is all; once the understanding is present *you may do what you like.*"

These words may convey to the uninitiated the feeling that once there is the understanding, the individual has the freedom to perpetrate any evil and scandalous deed. This would be an entirely erroneous interpretation. It is the reason why Jnaneshwar and other sages forbid such knowledge being propounded to all and sundry in a public place. There is also another reason. Such knowledge is to be given to those few — a spiritually evolved elite minority of seekers — who could be trusted to keep the game going and not spoil it. The show must go on, the totality of manifestation and its functioning, "the cosmic game of hide-and-seek, of God not letting his right hand know what his left hand is doing."

How does a truly deep understanding of the two-sidedness of the One actually work for the seeker? The first stage is an "expansion" of consciousness (though consciousness neither expands nor contracts) which represents the overcoming of the covering of ignorance (veil of *maya*) that has brought about the appearance of multiplicity and otherness. This means that the seeker has transcended himself as a separate individual by his new awareness of his true nature. At this stage he sees through the game and is almost ready to opt himself out of the game because the game is not worth the effort. Who is almost ready to opt out? Obviously, it is the residue of the old ego-subject which is inebriated with its new discovery. As Buddha, at this stage, exclaimed, "O builder, I have discovered thee! Never shalt though rebuild this fabric! Now the rafters are all shattered and the ridge-pole lies broken!" Perhaps this moment is supposed to correspond with the *pralaya* (the final dissolution of the universe), when conceptualization ceases with the discovery that the manifested universe is an illusion.

But the Advaitic philosophy goes much deeper. It *accepts* the illusoriness of the manifested universe (including the human individual) — the transcendence aspect — but at the same time, does not prevent the illusory individual from continuing with the game. The seeker who has become the sage must continue to play the game of hide and seek, good against evil, success against failure. He plays in the full knowledge that it is a game. He knows that the apparent manifested universe, although illusory like the shadow, can be present only because it is sustained by the immanent Absolute. In other words, the transcendent aspect of the manifestation (the illusoriness) goes along with the immanent aspect. The illusoriness is the objective aspect of the absolute subject. The manifested universe is, of course, an illusion. But that illusion could not have appeared by itself without the ground of the absolute unmanifest. The manifestation is certainly present but that presence is an appearance on the consciousness. The moving pictures certainly appear, but they could not have appeared in the absence of the screen on which they appear. So, the enlightened sage has become free of the bondage of the opposites.

> Content with getting what arrives of itself
> Passed beyond the pairs, free from envy,

*Not attached to success nor failure,*
*Even acting, he is not bound.*

*Bhagavad Gita*

It should be clear by now that the problems by which the individual human considers himself beset are based on the belief that the opposites are supposed to be separated and kept apart, that the good and the beautiful must be sought to the absolute exclusion of all that is considered evil and ugly. "Freedom from the pairs", however, is what freedom truly means. Our effort to separate one pole of a magnet from the other can only mean breaking the magnet itself. The "freed" sage is no longer interested in manipulating the opposites so as to choose one from the other. He is content to accept both as the very basis of life. He fully understands that what-is, is not good against evil, not life against death. There is a center of attention, an awareness that witnesses and transcends both.

This freedom from pairs is the kingdom of Heaven spoken of in the Bible, even though most of the exegetists seem to have forgotten it. Heaven is not the state of all positive virtues and rewards to the exclusion of all negative items, but the state of transcendence of both positives and negatives.

According to the Gospel of St. Thomas:

*They said to Him:*
*Shall we then, being children, enter the Kingdom?*
*Jesus said:*
*When you make the two one, and*
*when you make the inner as the outer*
*and the outer as the inner*
*and the above as the below,*
*and when you make the male and the female*
*into a single one*
*then you shall enter the Kingdom.*

It is well-known that this idea of "no-two-ness" is the essence of the philosophy of Advaita (non-duality) and also of Mahayana Buddhism. The *Lankavatara Sutra* says:

> *False imagination teaches that such things as light and shade, long and short, black and white, are different and are to be discriminated; but they are not independent of each other; they are only different aspects of the same thing; they are terms of relation, not of reality. Conditions of existence are not of a mutually exclusive character; in essence things are not two but one.*

In other words, ultimate reality, the unmanifest, is *Unicity*. For the purpose of manifesting itself objectively, Unicity must necessarily use the instrumentation or mechanics of duality (as the various pairs of interrelated opposites). The essential reality is the unmanifest, unaware of itself. Manifestation occurs as an appearance in consciousness simultaneously and concurrently with the arising of the conscious thought "I Am". Therefore what has appeared as a manifestation cannot be other than the unmanifest reality. That which *appears* in Consciousness is some thing that is sensed by the senses and is perceived and cognized as form, sound, odor, taste and touch. When we distinguish one thing from another, we do so because each thing has been given a name in order to discriminate between them. Such discrimination is necessary only so that communication may be possible between man and man. When it is realized that the essential reality of each thing and all things would continue to remain the same even if the name and form of every thing is suddenly changed, discrimination as such ceases. What remains is seen as the true essence of *all* things, including the human, — and this is called in Mahayana Buddhism the *"Suchness" of Reality*. As the *Lankavatara Sutra* says, this universal, undifferentiated inscrutable "Suchness" is the only reality. It is also the "Void" because it is void of all thought and therefore of all things.

The theory of quantum mechanics has demolished the notion of basically separated objects, and the Eastern Sage has always been talking of "all in one and one in all". The essence of what the Eastern Sage has been saying and what the physicist now confirms is not a great mystery. In one's immediate attention or awareness there are no boundaries, no separate items of manifestation, unless and until there is specific concentration on a particular item. To put it another way, one's visual field at any moment in time is "a kaleidoscopic flux of all sorts of interwoven patterns and textures, a mix of tree plus sky plus grass plus ground, and waves plus sand plus rocks and clouds...". One does not see any particular item as a single separate thing until thought intrudes and directs the attention to a separate thing, i.e. a pretty girl, or a striking combination of attire or an unusual event or whatever. In other words, our normal vision is total. It does not have any separation, any bondage, any boundaries until thought or conceptualization intrudes and *creates* the separateness. This in turn gives rise to a whole chain of other thoughts and reactions. That is to say, it is conceptualization that creates separation between the pairs as well as between objects and events, which in turn leads to conflict and unhappiness.

The realization that boundaries are a product of thought is at once the realization that the separation caused by these boundaries and the conflicts that ensue are *all* illusory. Conflicts are caused by thought and trying to get rid of these conflicts by further thought is like trying to "wash off blood with blood." Merely seeing that the conflict and the unhappiness is not real but illusory is the only way to *dissolve the problem.* Trying to solve it by further thinking and positive doing is merely making the matter worse. To this may be added one very valid observation: the basis of almost all thought (other than the thinking on technical problems) is the individual — the "me" — and there just does not exist such a creature!

This idea of oneness, propounded now by both the sage and the physicist alike, appears most frustrating to those who have been brought up for centuries on the ideal of "making the world a better place" — a world of pleasure without pain, health without sickness, wealth without poverty, success without failure, and indeed life without death! It strikes at the very root of all that their life stands for. Their ideal is based on the very concept that makes for conflict and unhappiness, i.e. their linear (as distinct from cyclic) view of time and history. What the idea of one-without-a-second means is the annihilation of the ego-subject, or the mind, or the individual (they are all synonyms). The supposed individual may well be excused if he considers the idea of oneness without separateness as being analogous to cutting off the head to cure a persistent headache. It is difficult to accept that the answer to the individual's unhappiness and misery is the annihilation of the individual himself! The annihilation of the individual really means disidentification with the object with which there is identification. It means disidentification of the subjectivity (which every human being is) from the projected phenomenal self-hood. Consciousness *as such* is all that "one" is. This conviction leads to what may be called a "noumenal living", disidentified from the phenomenal object. Living noumenally means being in non-objective relation with all things. Being in non-objective relation with all things means living without volition. Living without volition means ceasing to objectify. Living in pure thought ("I Am") prior to "name and form" means merely witnessing (without reaction) all events which are indeed "moved only by the Will of God". This is what disidentification means. Identification means separation and conflict.

The philosophy that has been outlined is, it must be firmly stated, not just a theory that "sounds" good. It is indeed a working philosophy in the sense that its strength lies not in its words but in the active practice of it. The significant point is that in trying to make the world a better place than it is, the immediate presumption is that that power which created the world is now in a position of utter helplessness. Where God has failed, mighty man must now take over because in the absence of man's individual and collective effort, the world has become chaos. The point is conveniently forgotten that man has been trying to improve the world for the last several hundred years and if there is chaos as man sees it, it is man himself who is responsible. There are two aspects to this matter. One is that man has himself created the horrific problems which face mankind today (including the clear possibility of total annihilation through nuclear weapons) and is now feverishly trying to atone for it — by creating more and more terrible weapons in order to deter the "enemy" from using them! This is in itself almost a slapstick comedy situation. The other aspect, a more subtle one, is that it is no use blaming anyone for the present situation.  The discovery of the theory of relativity by Albert Einstein was not the creation of Einstein's brain. He himself has gone on record to say that the formula came to him "from outside". For the formula to have come from outside ("outside" must obviously mean universal Mind or Consciousness) a brain had to be evolved which had the *capacity* to receive what was offered; which means a brain that was evolved *by nature* over a period of time.  That the process of evolution culminated in a particular psychosomatic organism named "Albert Einstein" is almost an irrelevancy. Would it not seem, if the matter is considered from this viewpoint, that the individual human with his puny brain (donated through the courtesy of nature) is presumptuous beyond measure in either taking credit or blame for the existing state of the world?

If this is clearly understood, it will also be comprehended why it seems the more we try to control the world, the faster it runs away from us. The fact of the matter is that we have separated ourselves from the universe with its unimaginably complex system of relationship. The more we collect and try to understand its details, the more it eludes us — by slyly revealing yet more details to study. Indeed, it is a game of hide and seek, — the *lila* of universal Consciousness in the functioning of its total manifestation!

It is only when the individual views the universe as inseparable from himself that he sees everything in perspective. Then, as did Lao Tzu, he can say, "I know the whole universe without leaving my house". What is significant is, that once this view of the universe becomes deeply ingrained in one's being, one truly understands "the winds, the tides, the currents, the seasons, and the principles of growth and decay". Then one's actions flow with them and not against them because the whole principle of this working philosophy is "going with the grain". The secret of the real apprehension of this philosophy is that technology becomes destructive only when this oneness of the universe is not understood. And — even more significantly — the not understanding of the oneness of the universe is also part of the What-Is! The latter aspect of the apperception is important. It must be realized not only that problems are created because conscious attention and linear thinking has upset the basic principles (and the rhythm and pulse of the natural process) of the universal working, but that, at the same time, this situation itself is part of the functioning of Totality. The understanding of the problem means the dissolution of the problem and of the accompanying distress: "What-Is" is precisely what God wants at this present moment.

The key to the relationship between opposites is what is known in Taoist philosophy as "mutual arising". Like the opposite but inseparable sides of a coin, or the pulse and interval in vibration, the very existence of one is dependent on the other. There cannot be any question of a conflict between the two because the two opposites really are more like lovers in passionate embrace than enemies in mortal combat. Indeed, the original interrelated opposites are beingness and non-beingness. But for most people, the very concept of non-beingness is frightening because they consider it as the final and permanent end of everything including "themselves". They fail to realize that the imagined void is not emptiness but fullness of potential out of which arises the beingness. "Being" can only come out of "non-being", precisely as sound can only come out of silence and light from darkness. Could it be that the terror of the void arises from the fact that it cannot be made intelligible in terms of material bodies? The fact of the matter is that it is "almost impossible to give intelligible descriptions of elements or dimensions which are constant in all experiences, i.e. consciousness, time, motion or electricity." In regard to electricity, for example, it is interesting to note what the *Encyclopedia Britannica* has to say:

> Today, however, we find that the phenomena of electricity cannot be so explained, and the tendency is to explain all other phenomena in terms of electricity, taken as a fundamental thing. The question, "What is electricity?" is essentially *unanswerable, if by it is sought an explanation of the nature of electricity in terms of material bodies* (italics added).

The "mutually arising" order of natural forces can be seen in the way Chinese philosophy conceives the five energies as symbolized by *wood*, which is the fuel which gives rise to *fire*, which creates ash and gives rise to *earth*, which in its mines contains *minerals* which (like the surface of a metal mirror) attracts dew, giving rise to *water*, which in turn nourishes *wood*.

This cyclical view of the working of forces is seen in the *yin-yang* view of the duality in the world and gives rise to the serene "attitude of respectful trust towards nature and human nature". This can be seen in the old story of a farmer whose horse ran away:

> When the neighbors came to sympathize with him, he said, "Bad luck? May be". The next day the horse returned and brought with it six wild horses. The neighbors promptly congratulated him on his good fortune. He

said, "Good luck? May be". Then, the following day, when his son tried to saddle and ride
one of the wild horses, he fell and broke his leg.
When the neighbors came to commiserate
with him on his misfortune, the farmers
answer once more was, "May be". The day
after that, the conscription officers came to the
village and took all the young men for the
army, but the farmer's son was rejected because of his broken leg. To the neighbors who
had again gathered and said, "Everything
turned out well after all," he answered, "May
be."

This is the serene attitude that is most likely to follow a
deep understanding of the polarity of opposites and the
basic non-duality in the universe. It is not an attitude of
pessimism and hopelessness, but rather one of serene acceptance of the fact that fortune and misfortune, sickness
and health come and go. Constant change *is* life and life is
change. The error lies not in nature but in the attitude
which demands that the course of nature halt at a particular
moment of well-being. The fact of the matter is that you *are*
the everlasting unchanging moment and merely *witness* the
*lila* of changing relationships that we call life. It is a matter
of realizing that the individual is very much a part of the
manifestation and its process of functioning. There is no
way he can, as an individual, get himself out of that process.
It is a matter of apperceiving that the universe is "a multi-
dimensional network of jewels, each one containing the
reflections of all the others *ad infinitum*". Each jewel represents a "thing-event" and there is no obstruction between
one thing-event and another. Thing-events take place according to their allotted function. The supposed volition of
the supposed individual is altogether irrelevant. The
whole cosmos is implicit unicity, although expressed in
explicit duality. Therefore, every point in the cosmos must
necessarily be considered as its center. It is almost impos-

sible to describe the sense of magnificence that comes out of an apperception of the nature of the individual in relation to the manifestation. *The loss of individuality is exchanged for the gain of the totality of the cosmos.*

What does the true comprehension of the polarity of opposites ultimately mean? It means being aware of what actually *Is*, without getting involved in an effort to measure it, judge it, or give it a specific name or label. It means *being* an intrinsic part of that reality of "What-Is" instead of merely having a concept about it. Often the objection is raised that it is impossible to suppress the flush of thoughts and ideas, and the babble of words that arise almost simultaneously with the perceiving. True, but is this not also part of the "What-Is" at that moment, and therefore merely a part of the "What-Is" to be aware about? The point is not really to ignore or suppress the thoughts and ideas that arise, but merely to be aware of them as part of the What-Is. You ask, "What happens then?" What would then happen is that instead of the horizontal proliferation of the thoughts and words, followed by the reaction of futility and frustration, (further followed by a mental dialogue), the calm awareness, or the witnessing, of the "What-Is" would vertically cut off such horizontal proliferation. Indeed, the arising of the horizontal involvement in thought and the vertical cutting off of such involvement would, in the beginning, happen at frequent intervals. But, gradually, the witnessing — the awareness without judgement — would take over. The intervals between involvements would become longer and longer until, suddenly, there would be the realization that awareness has become a steady phenomenon like a continuous stream of oil being poured out.

# The Individual And His Mind

The individual and *his* mind! Any thinking based on the premise that the individual is an entity and that he has a mind of his own, is bound to lead to grave intellectual problems and dead-ends.

What is the individual human as an object? What is it that makes him basically and essentially different from an inanimate object, such as an automobile or a chimpanzee, (man's closest relative)? In other words, if we consider the human individual as a machine and as an ape, in what area do we look for the fundamental distinction? Surely it must be in the area of the "mind" that we must find the distinction. At one time the individual believed that spirits and humors inhabited the body — he loved with his "heart" and he could not "stomach" certain things — but science soon made it clear that the heart is a mere pump and the stomach a chemical factory. The result was that the spirits, thus exorcised, "went straight to our heads, like bats to the belfry." And now the individual human makes frantic efforts to discover himself, to discover his true nature "in the vast machinery of our brain or in the unique abilities and predilections we call our mind."

It is almost impossible to think of "mind" without its physical representation, which is the "brain". In fact the two words are, more often than not, used as synonyms. Steve Levy gives his reaction to his finding Einstein's brain as follows: "I had risen up to look into the jar, but now I was sunk in my chair, speechless. My eyes were fixed on that jar as I tried to comprehend that these pieces of gunk bubbling up and down had caused a revolution in physics and quite possibly, changed the course of civilization. There it was".

Indeed, there it is — the tragic misconception that the brain, the physical matter, could produce the essential thought which was the basis of the revolution. Einstein has stated quite unequivocally that the equation "came from outside". He obviously meant that his "individual" thinking did not lead him to the equation but that his brain was capable of *receiving* the equation which "came from outside." The Totality of Functioning — what the Buddhist calls the Mind (with a capital M) and what the Advaitin calls Consciousness — needed a brain that would be capable of receiving the gift of the equation, and it happened to be the Einstein brain that was evolved over a period. To consider that it was a superior individual human, called Albert Einstein, who "created" the equation in his brain is to miss the point altogether.

The human brain is nothing but three pounds or so of living tissues, made up of "blood vessels, some membranous linings, some fluid-filled cavities, and many billions of specialized cells, the most important of which are about ten billion neurons". Together they form a communications network of unbelievable complexity. The brain is the operating center of the body and is in charge of overseeing all the vital processes in the psychosomatic apparatus. It must be realized that this operating center cannot function without the necessary "energy of life", *the animus*, which comes from Consciousness (the knowledge "I Am"). The operating center in the brain imparts a sense of oneness to the various parts of the body, and more importantly, a sense of separate selfhood. The realization that our true nature is not the operating center but the functional center (the animating Consciousness which is common to all individual bodies) is what is generally understood as Self-realization or enlightenment. Indeed, what this Self-realization amounts to is the apperception that all that exists is Consciousness (which provides sentience — and life itself — to *all* sentient objects), and that human beings are mere objects without any separate autonomous existence. If electricity is turned off at the source, all objects depending for their existence on electricity would cease to function. Likewise, if sentience were to be turned off by that supreme Source (called God or any other name like the Absolute or Consciousness) from which has emanated this manifestation, all human beings and other objects would cease to be.

In regard to the nature of the mind, Ramana Maharshi, the sage of Arunachala, has explained that the mind is nothing other than the "me"-thought. The "you" and the "he" — the second and the third person pronouns — arise only after the first person "me" appears. The mind and the ego are one and the same, and the intellect and the memory (the collection of mental tendencies) are all the one mind. The different names are similar to the different appellations given to the different functions of the same person. The individual human is nothing but this ego. This means that it is erroneous and fallacious to think that there is an individual self which functions through the body and the mind. The "me" as an individual self is a mental modification. Actually, there is no such thing as mind apart from thought. It is because of the emergence of thought that a source of thought is conceived and is termed as "mind". When the source of thought is probed *continuously as it arises*, it is clearly found that there is no such thing as mind.

When this is not clearly understood, one tries to seek the connection between the brain and the mind, and lands oneself in utter confusion and futile controversies. To a certain extent, the concept of mind as the source of thought, a thing instead of an activity in relation to the brain, is based on the conditioning that every noun must be a thing endowed with some permanence and with an enduring aspect of its own. But in this kind of thinking it is forgotten or ignored that the "me" today is not really the "me" that was some time ago because dying cells are all the time being replaced by new ones, and the matter making up a cell is spent and replaced. But then, even the almost inevitable conclusion, that mind is an aspect or function of the physical brain, is not truly acceptable. Even if we did know the entire mechanism of the brain (which we do not know today) that is supposed to give rise to the mind, we cannot conceive *any mechanism* giving rise to the mind. This is the problem which Schopenhauer calls the "world knot". Even if we did have full knowledge of how information filters in through the senses and gets processed, how memories are stored, skills learned and decisions made, and how our muscles, glands and all vital functions are controlled, we would perhaps still not know much about thoughts and sensations and their association with consciousness.

Where are thoughts made? This is the question that bothers — and humbles — the neuro-physician. Evidence and research concerning the construction and activity of the brain could easily mislead the scientist. He might believe that the individual — the knower — is only an effect of the activity of the billions of neurons in the brain communicating with one another, and that consciousness ceases to exist as soon as the brain ceases to act. A thought is a sensation that contains significant ingredients of memory into the past, a projection into the future, and sensory stimulations. What this means is that a verbal structure is created around certain phenomena and then a certain physical entity is attached to them. All kinds of questions arise if one begins to include thoughts in the dynamics of the body. Are thoughts then reducible to the past and present stimuli that are processed through our internal hormonal and neuronal computers? While the machine metaphor is useful to a certain extent when studying the functioning of various body parts including the brain, the fact remains that while there can be an unconditional release of *all* stored information in the case of a computer, there cannot be any such *transfer of information* between human individuals.

Man's fear of the void of death refers more to his own personal knowledge than anything else because that is what, for him, constitutes his individuality. This is what has led to the unprecedented assault, in the last fifteen years, on what constitutes "mind", and whether there is something called "self" independent of the brain. The intellectual drama contained in this search is further heightened by the acceptance by modern scientists that knowledge although "irrationally" acquired does have a value and that physical events defying physical "laws" do have validity. The entire discussion is based on the assumption that the human individual is an autonomic and independent entity with volition, and such discussion must go on until it is realized that the very assumption of the independence of the human individual is wholly illusory! The crux of the matter is in the questions: "Who (or what) is it that wants to know?" and "Is it possible for the mind to know its own source?"

It is interesting to note what physically constitutes the individuality or selfhood of the human object. The characteristic structural features of every human are determined by the inherited blueprint contained in the molecules of DNA (deoxyribonucleic acid) in which are combined both the actual and latent features from the two parents. Characteristics thought to be determined in this way include not only the physical features and stature, body type, and color of hair and eyes, but also perhaps such mental and emotional features such as a tendency towards artistic expression, ambition or lack of it, boldness or timidity, and others. This is at one end of the scale of structures constituting our bodies. At the other end of the scale, precise structures of large molecules are specified by the parental determinants. These are the nucleic acids (including DNA) which are the carriers of genetic information, and the proteins, such as the histocompatibility antigens, which define for each individual a unique self-hood (recognized as one's own by the immunity system that guards the individual against incursions by foreign bodies). The individuality of the proteins is wholly genetic while the individuality of the personal experiences belongs to the nervous system.

It would seem that while specifying most characteristics as the two ends of the structural scale, nature leaves the details in the middle range to be filled in by what must be called "chance". A viable organism would not be hampered in its functioning even if the intermediate details were not specified in the DNA blueprint. It would thus seem that nature shows its hand in the DNA blueprint but reserves a certain mystery for itself through "chance".

The early pictorial representations of the brain show some empty space set aside for the storage of past events (memory). In these representations there is a "front" memory (as with both humans and computers) limited in volume but quickly accessible, as contrasted with the peripheral memory, the reading of which is comparatively much slower. Since the days of Aristotle the idea had prevailed that events constituting experience leave their impression on the brain, starting with a blank page. Today we no longer believe in such a *tabula rasa* concerning the brain, and we accept that our born personalities contain a mixture of nature and experience, although the relative proportion may be a matter of dispute among the experts.

If it is accepted that memory is physical, it must necessarily have a location, and it was a young physiological psychologist named Karl S. Lashley, who started a hunt for the seat of memory in 1926. The culmination of this hunt, which lasted for almost twenty-five years, was his now famous paper "In Search of the Engram" in 1950. He did not find the location of the engram (the physical record), nor that of the learning mechanism in the brain, but he did find that for most complex tasks, involving perhaps several different senses, all parts of the neo-cortex made their individual contributions which were of almost equal value. He concluded therefore that any single event must necessarily involve the activity of perhaps millions of neurons scattered all over the neo-cortex  Since then the idea of a "distributed memory" has been the prevalent view. It is a view which has gained (substantial) support after the invention of the laser holograph in the early sixties — a scene recorded on photographic film appears, after due processing, in three dimensional form, as if the original object was standing in space.

Two more interesting aspects of the hologram are:

(1) that any small part of the film can be used to reproduce the entire scene, which means that the entire scene is contained in every part of the film or, that while every piece has a little bit about every other part, no piece is essential; and

(2) that one can superimpose any number of holograms on the same piece of film and then reproduce them separately one by one.

Brain theorists were, of course, greatly attracted to this case of distributed memory, and it has even been suggested that the whole world is a hologram  There are, of course, other scientists who do not attach all that much importance to the holographic theory of memory.  But such a theory would, to a large extent, explain the many mysteries of memories of "past lives", and more importantly, explain the evolutionary processes of the brain in case of prodigies and geniuses in every field of activity, whether it is an Einstein or a Mozart or a Jnaneshwar.

The precise dynamics of the brain are determined by the strength and distribution of the synopses, that is to say, by the trillions of connections made by the trillions of neurons in the human neo-cortex with one another.  It would seem from the vastness and precision of this structural mass that nothing in it is left to chance.  And yet we find considerable variability even in genetically identical neural structures (twins), which would indicate that the early effects of chance frozen into the infant brain would have a great deal to do with the memories that will be formed in due course.  In other words, *chance is turned into essence,* and this welding constitutes the unique individuality of each of the humans.  It is an individuality based not only on the DNA, but also a memory traced from perhaps millions of earlier holograms.  It would seem to be a clear indication that *nature brings about the required thought-pattern according to the needs of the evolutionary process* in every field of activity, maintaining a close interrelationship and unity in the mind-boggling diversity.

The question arises: What precisely is the position of the neo-cortex in the brain in regard to the thinking process: Is there a self-supporting "thinking cap" in the brain?  The neo-cortex, in spite of all the complexity in its structure and its privileged position in the brain, is not capable of thought.  It is the structure known as RAS, (reticular activating system) in the brainstem that allows thought.  Without it consciousness cannot exist, and permanent damage to it means instant, irreversible coma.  On the other hand, even extensive damage in the cortex will not impair consciousness because no single portion of it is essential for conscious activity. It would thus be difficult to accept the idea of an independent thinking center in the cortex. Moreover, there are two interesting phenomena which discount the *supreme* importance of the cortex. One is what the psychologists call "projection". This concerns the fact that an external event picked up by our senses is felt not at the receiving end but at the source. For instance, the ring of a bell is in the bell-tower and not in our brain. Second, there is a similar projection not in space but in time. Experiments clearly suggest that *as much as half a second elapses before we become conscious of an event picked up by our senses*. In other words, we are continuously living in the past!

What the spatial and durational projections bring out is the fact that we are not the imagined conscious self in a brain capsule but that *our cognitive selves are outside the body*. In other words, it means that perception and cognition extends well beyond the brain case. Brain cases are in fact mere recording instruments. Neils Bohr makes the suggestion that we do not even really know what the boundary of our observing self is: "We cannot even tell which particular molecules belong to a living organism." Would this not clearly point to the fact that Consciousness is not an individual "possession" but something universal and *out there* in which the world itself appears as a hologram?

An interesting sideline about this matter of the location of consciousness in any particular part of the body is what the great sage of modern times, Ramana Maharshi, said concerning the subject. He had always averred that the Heart is the center of the self, the supreme center, behind the *jiva* or the individual ego-self. This heart is not the physical heart on the left but something on the right, which cannot be known by the mind or realized by imagination. The only direct way to realize it is to cease to fantasize and be yourself. When there is realization, you intuitively *feel* that the center is there. He went on to say that he chanced upon a verse in the Malayalam version (one of the South Indian languages) of *Ashtangahridayam*, the standard work on the Hindu system of medicine called *Ayurveda*, wherein the *ojassthana* (source of physical energy or "place of light") is mentioned as being located in the right side of the chest and called the seat of Consciousness (*samvit*). It seemed odd that the Maharshi should have fixed a place for the Heart, thereby implying physiological limitations to Consciousness which metaphysically is beyond space and time. But he made it clear that the answer was in reference to a question by a person who had identified himself with his body. He asked the questioner: "While putting the question now, would you say that your body alone is here but that you are speaking from somewhere else?"

From the metaphysical point of view, it must be clearly understood that pure Consciousness is truly indivisible, without shape or form, without any "within" or "without". From this absolute standpoint, the Heart, as the "seat" of Consciousness cannot have any specific place assigned to it in the physical body. In the true perspective, Consciousness is all that exists — every sentient being *feels* "I am" — and the physical bodies of the sentient beings are the instruments through which Consciousness expresses itself objectively. It is similar to the way in which electricity (as an aspect of the energy that is Consciousness) expresses itself through various objects and gadgets.

Says Alfred North Whitehead, "....But the mind, in apprehending, also experiences sensations which, properly speaking, are qualities of the mind alone. These sensations are projected by the mind so as to clothe appropriate bodies in external nature. Thus the bodies are perceived as with qualities which in reality do not belong to them, qualities which are in fact purely the offspring of the mind. Thus nature gets credit which should in truth be reserved for ourselves: the rose for its scent, the nightingale for its song, the sun for its radiance...Nature is a dull affair, soundless, scentless, colorless; merely the hurrying of material endlessly, meaninglessly." What Whitehead means is that a mind that could apprehend an object, *as it truly is* (without any modification or error), would know precisely nothing at all. This is the whole-mind of the *jnani* or the sage.

There are processes which go beyond the concept of the sensory-motor. They include both sensory inputs modified by the manipulative mind without necessarily leading to motor action and also motor actions that emerge spontaneously or as a result of cerebral activity (thought). There is a clear distinction between mere "seeing" and "perceiving". What actually happens is that instead of merely "seeing" — which is a process of information flow from the receptors to the brain — the LGN (lateral geniculate nucleus), the simple relay station, gets transformed into a filtering place where the message from the eyes gets mixed with the echo from the cortex: "Seeing" becomes "perceiving" through the process of the cortex reaching out to the periphery, to intercept the incoming messages. *It then filters and alters with its own input.* Fact and fancy become interwoven on this "internal retina". The extent to which this interweaving of fact and fancy happens is astonishing. There is a phenomenon known as "pattern completion", whereby omissions or defects of visual patterns or recorded sentences go quite unnoticed, and the subjects carry on as if they had seen the whole visual pattern or heard the entire sentence. What has happened is that *the mind has interpreted reality by modifying it*: the split mind of the ordinary individual has been at work.

What this means is that there is a correlation between the fantasizing mind and sensory control. There is the obvious need in life for a balance because the excess of one could mean being adrift with dreams and hallucinations, while the excess of the other could mean pedestrian and unimaginative perceptions. A slightly hazy picture can give rise to various interpretations, while a too sharply focussed one can deaden the sensibility. A painting with all objects sharply shown, irrespective of the distance between them, gives the impression of unreality as compared to one done in perspective.

There is another aspect to the subject of perception, whereby it is believed that perception is a direct process involving a minimum of cerebral activity. Thus James J. Gibson of Cornell University in his "Theory of Affordances", talks of affordances "being considered as intrinsic in the stimulus, e.g. a rigid object with a sharp dihedral angle, an edge, affords cutting and scraping — it is a knife." Also, in gestalt psychology, the properties of every perceived object are supposed to be contained in the direct stimulus engendered by the object: thus, a fruit says, "eat me", thunder and lightening says "fear me", and woman says, "love me".

It would seem that both points of view have some relevance at some time or the other, in some circumstances or other. The fact however, remains that when an object evokes an unusually strong reaction of conflict or emotion, perception may not remain as direct perception because the immediate, direct perception could well be manipulated to an extent which totally distorts the direct perception. This is what makes a philosopher say that everything is in the mind.

It is often not realized that perception does not mean the operation necessarily of only one of the senses. More often than not, it involves the simultaneous involvement of several senses. A breeze on one's face is felt because of various skin sensors; simultaneously you hear it and also see it as movement in the leaves of a tree or on the surface of water. So, most of the events in everyday life are perceived as combinations of various sensations called sensory schemata. If any one of these is absent, the mind makes every effort to compensate for that absence because otherwise the perception would seem unreal and disturbing, e.g. a howling storm outside seen from an air-conditioned, sound-proof room.

A look at the efferent side of the brain shows that sensors are contained in every part of the apparatus of action (the muscles, the tendons, the joints), and conversely the somatosensory cortex (the locus of our body sensations) borders on and probably "talks" across to the motor cortex. In other words, actions produce sensations just as certainly as sensations cause actions. Indeed, the very thought of an action brings about the associated sensations: "a train of thought generally contains both of these ingredients...in continuous feedback, one reinforcing the other." It is for this reason that the spiritual seeker is asked to resort to *witnessing* or *being consciously aware of* the very first thought (after a gap of the absence of thought). The object is to cut off the train of thought that inevitably arises, thereby constituting what is called conceptualizing or objectivizing. Such witnessing is not of the mind but outside of it. The train of thought is a horizontal sequence of thoughts leading to sensation or action which in its turn gives rise to further thinking. Witnessing is a vertical operation which cuts off this horizontal sequence. If the horizontal sequence is not cut off it could result in a runaway situation, as in the case of mental disturbance. Normally, however, each sequence of thoughts gets cut off when new and different sense impressions stream in and demand the attention of the central nervous system.

Perhaps the most significant factor in the formation of a self-image (the "me"), is the factor of volition (freedom of will). The basis of most Eastern religions is the belief, even the faith, that it is only God (or by whatever word the absolute principle is called) who determines the destiny of every man in the world. Even the western religions have, as their basis, the basic principle, "Not me, but Thou, O Lord". And it is this deep faith in predetermination which leads so many men, otherwise known for their independent thinking, to fortune tellers to learn what the future holds for them. If they truly believed that they hold their future in their own hands, they would never deign to go to a fortune teller. On the other hand, the Eastern man believes that his fate has already been determined when he was born, and yet believes in *karma*, the basis of which is volition! It is this kind of double-bind which makes the concept of volition into the tremendous problem that it has been for such a long period of time.

The materialist scientist of the nineteenth century would consider the human being as a machine, strictly subject to absolute, deterministic physical laws: "the outcome of human actions should be determined by the state of the machine and the stimuli impinging on it; free will must therefore be a delusion". Apart from a stubborn minority, few scientists today would accept this approach, although several biologists do believe that science will ultimately be able "to reduce physical processes to predictable phenomena". There is, on the other hand, the dualist tradition which introduces the concept of a kind of "internal psychokinesis" in order to explain that freedom of will is achieved by the "mind", a "conscious non-physical entity, separate and *independent of the brain*," able to influence the brain and thus express its will. Sir John Eccles attempts to meet some serious difficulties with known physical laws by having the circuits of neurons in the brain so delicately poised that only a minute influence is needed for the desired effect to be produced. Still, the influence would be non-physical.

There is, of course, an inherent paradox in the traditional concept of freedom itself. There is supposed to be freedom only if actions are determined by drives and motivations, and such freedom is considered as being restricted if an external disturbance interferes with them. According to the dualist, the undisturbed functioning of the brain cannot be considered to be free because it is predetermined by its own inherent dynamics, including needs, drives, etc. This problem is worse confounded when the dualist imposes another will on the brain, which in effect means the body's freedom is freedom from itself. The only way to resolve this dilemma is to ask: for whom is this dilemma? And then we pass on to the field of metaphysics.

As the sage Ramana Maharshi puts it, destiny is the result of past action. Cause becomes effect which in turn becomes the cause of further effect. The Maharshi endorsed: "Let the body act as may suit it. Why are you concerned with it? Why do you pay attention to it?" Whatever happens is the result of past actions, of divine will and of other factors. In regard to free will, he says that there is a sense of enjoyment and of individual will only so long as there is a sense of doership. If this sense of doership is lost, it will be the divine will which will be seen as the one to guide the course of events. A specific question was put by a visitor, "Can it be that it was already decided that on such and such a day, at such and such and hour, I should move this hand fan in this manner, and then put it down here?" The Maharshi's answer was, "Certainly. Whatever this body is to do and whatever experiences it is to pass through was already decided when it came into existence." That was certainly clear, precise and without any equivocality.

Perhaps the matter will be seen in greater clarity if we consider a tricky question that was put to Ramana Maharshi: "If what is destined to happen will happen, is there any purpose in prayer or effort, or should we just remain actionless?".

The answer was:

> "There are only two ways to conquer destiny or be independent of it. One is to enquire for whom is this destiny and discover that only the ego is bound by destiny and not the Self, that the ego is nonexistent. The other way is to kill the ego by completely surrendering to the Lord, by realizing one's helplessness and thinking all the time, 'Not I but thou, O, Lord', giving up all sense of me and leaving it to the Lord to do what He likes with you."

It is rather a curious fact that the human being greatly values what he considers as the "freedom to act", in which sense the will is motivational, based on memories, associations, emotions, questions of ethics and projections into the future. And yet he is never without some discomfort, some mental unease, concerning what might have been if the decision were different. Indeed, his doubt extends to the question whether in identical circumstance he would again make the same decision and act the same way. The fact of the matter is that it is almost impossible that the circumstances could be recreated in all details and that there would be the same options to choose from. The recreation of a past set of alternatives has been called "contra-factual fallacy", that is to say, against the facts as they prevail. Therefore, such thinking is merely an exercise in futility, "the never-failing vice of fools", as Alexander Pope put it. Perhaps, in considering the question of freedom of the will or choice, it would be wise to restrict our role in the decision-making process to merely that of witnessing!

It is an interesting fact that the actions of a human being at any moment would appear to be caused not by his *conscious* participation *at that moment*, but by the memory of what he thought and felt in the past. Benjamin Libet, a noted neurophysician, determined through a set of experiments that the instant at which a subject is able to respond to a stimulus by an action of his own is not necessarily the time at which he becomes conscious of the event. He found that it takes up to about half a second for a stimulus to produce a response (during which time some form of neural reverberation continues). Therefore, *actual sensations "are replays of events that are well in the past,* but manage to convey to us the delusion of a conscious immediacy and participation."* The significance of this fact is startling: we are living not in the present as we think but in the past. It follows that there is no present at all but only a shadow of what is already past What is more, what we think of as future will have become the past before we are aware of it. Life would thus seem to be "a grandiose hoax", unless we accept the metaphysical view of space-time as only a concept and not some *thing* to which we are bound as slaves.

It is rather a curious fact that physics, which has traditionally shown a clear bias towards the objective qualities of the universe (those which, upon measurement, yield the same values for any observer), should have, in recent times, "forced us into dilemmas in which it is almost impossible to maintain the neat separation between the observer and the observed". What this means is that the human being observing a part of nature as an observer, becomes part of the very *dynamics* of what he observes. This clear shift from Edington's view of life as "an insignificant and very local accident in the universe" to that of John Wheeler who speaks of the "universe of mind and man", is due very largely to the part played in modern physics by "quantum mechanics", which has something quite startling to tell us about the human mind. What has in fact happened is that the matter of the scale of things and the question of unpredictability invading many macroscopic events in the "classical regime" has now been further complicated by the character of self-reference and quantum mechanics. *The mere fact of observing affects what is being observed!*

The microworld is *inherently* chaotic, that is to say, unpredictable. A little bit of matter, barely visible under the microscope and suspended in a gas, is seen to go through jerky totally unpredictable motions that result from the random movements of the gas molecules. This is wholly in agreement with the Vedantic postulate that the smallest particle in the universe is in constant movement, as if in a dance (hence the mythical Dance of Shiva). If the macroscopic world appears relatively stable, ordered and reasonably predictable, it is because of the immense separation in scale. The unpredictability of the microcosm is averaged out into insignificance by the sheer magnitude in the macrocosm. Nonetheless, "there may be cross talk between the two realms and as a result microscopic uncertainty can be injected into the macroscopic world."

Human beings have come to expect the kind of stability seen in the earth's near-circular orbit around the sun, in other physical systems as well. Perhaps this is because physicists have so far concentrated their efforts on those systems which have well-behaved dynamics. But the intractables, such as the trajectories of tumbling dice, have been swept under the scientific carpet, and not much has been said about the so-called "chaotic systems". It is, however, becoming increasingly more apparent that chaotic systems are the rule in nature and not exceptions. They are all, in the classical sense, ordinary mechanical systems but "the dynamics are continually poised on knife-edge decisions whose outcome cannot be predicted." The microworld of ceaselessly moving molecules would seem to provide fluctuations which are sufficient to intrude on large-scale phenomena in the case of the very delicately poised chaotic systems; and thus it would appear that our ignorance of the microworld must extend to the macroworld.

When one speaks or thinks about oneself (self-reference), one does not realize that this "me", this self, is "forever imaging itself and changing in response to the image". And to the extent that it can never catch up with itself, it must necessarily remain undefined. The interesting part of this imaging process is that the imaging can and does take place very often not only from one's viewpoint but also from that of another, especially if the latter happens to be an opponent. And this is made even more interesting because both persons are under the same process of imaging, as in the case of poker game adversaries. What this kind of "reflexive dynamics" does in many cases is to bring about a special kind of indeterminacy because "as we keep going around the loops (structural loops contained in the human brain), the light of logic dims rapidly and becomes less and less compelling; where we stop in our chain of reasoning and where the opponent stops are thus fundamentally unpredictable."

The following is an extract from a New York Times editorial about the nuclear "balance of terror" between the Superpowers:

> If we think *they* might launch a first strike on military targets, why shouldn't they think we might, particularly if we "stress" our capacity for selective strikes? And if both sides think that of the other, isn't one ultimately likely to try it before the other can?"

What the matter truly boils down to is the question: What is the nature of the selfhood, the nature of the "me" that contemplates itself, seeks or avoids itself? Is the whole thing merely a concept? Is it a product of its own self-contemplation, the work of a bootstrap process that can create something out of nothing? The Indian mystic has, for the last several thousand years been expressing what he has intuitively seen: that the manifest universe is an appearance which has spontaneously arisen in Consciousness out of the unmanifest because that is its nature, that the unmanifest is a state of beingness in which the static Consciousness is not aware of itself, and that the manifest universe arises spontaneously along with the movement in Consciousness when the unmanifest suddenly becomes aware of itself with the arising of the thought "I Am". Now, modern science, out of its own tortuous processes, seems to have come to the same conclusion. In what John Wheeler has called "self-reference cosmogony", the origin of the universe is seen as the result of a singular event, "the big bang (the arising of "I Am"), the umbilicus of everything that exists. But, unlike other big bang theories, Wheeler's universe is a *"self-excited system"*. In it, past, present and future are "wired together" in such a way that its birth is not released "until the blind accidents of evolution are guaranteed to produce, for some non-zero stretch of time in its history-to-be, the consciousness and consciousness of consciousness, and communicating community, that will give meaning to that universe from start to finish." The end of the universe is foreseen by Wheeler dramatically as a collapse leading not to some continued dynamics that may deny life but very simply a sudden end, like smoke, figuratively speaking, rising from a machine at the critical moment. Suffice it to say that in Wheeler's cosmology — like that of some other scientists — consciousness is assigned a decisive role in the scheme of things. When the movement ceases, the manifested universe "collapses" in the consciousness in which it appeared.

Quantum mechanics is the most significant development in recent years to add to the traditional sources of confusion, chaos and uncertainty. Quantum mechanics is not just a capricious flight of imagination but an inevitable development, grounded on firm basis and almost compelled by incontrovertible, undeniable facts. The theory grew out of the realization that waves such as light waves,

X-rays, and others, whilst having all the characteristics of waves, behave like particles under certain circumstances. In 1925, the French physicist de Broglie proposed the view that particles such as electrons may also have the properties of waves. And very soon, these "matter waves" were actually found in the laboratory. Finally, Schroedinger proposed a new type of mechanics appropriate to these entities that combine particle and wave properties, which came to be known as "quantum mechanics."

Among the concepts that emerged from this revolutionary theory one of the best known is Heisenberg's "uncertainty principle." According to this, "particles move with an *inherent* fuzziness which allows us to specify only their probable locations, not where they *really* are." What is even more startling is the emphatic proposition by Niels Bohr and others (the Copenhagan School), that the uncertainties are not merely an inadequate knowledge or understanding but that they concern nature itself. In brief, what the theory tells us is that if an object has, say, a 40% chance of being in one place and 60% chance of being in another, the deciding factor is the observer himself. In other words, the observing "has not just recorded reality, *it has changed reality*." According to Eugene Wignes, this strange reaction between the observer and the observed object, has occurred "upon the entering of impressions into the consciousness."

The "classical" observations have been compared to looking through an underwater port of heavy plate glass at underwater marine life. The quantum mechanics theory says that the observer does not really peer unobtrusively through a plate of glass, but actually "manipulates and participates" in whatever he describes, and thereby brings about *unavoidable* and generally unpredictable changes, through the peculiar interaction between the observer's consciousness and the material reality that is observed. In other words, the result is decided one way or the other only when the observer has had a look at the matter, and it is quite senseless to say that the situation would have been the same if unobserved.

All this is quite contrary to what our common sense tells us. It says something must be one way or another, it cannot be both ways! A large number of experiments, however, clearly point to the fact that common sense is not to be depended upon, and that nature happens to be stranger than what we would expect it to be. And yet, is the quantum mechanics conclusion truly so strange? Is it strange that an interconnectedness should exist between things and events? Is it so difficult to conceive that the entire universe is bound into one intimate unit comprising the material manifestation and consciousness together with the mind (which is the content of consciousness)? Is this not precisely what the Indian mystics have been saying for years and years? Is this not precisely what is conveyed by the ancient Chinese saying, "You pull out a blade of grass and you shake the universe"? Is it not, therefore, logical that the new physics should "draw the observer on to the stage as an active participant in the spectacle his senses pick up"? Does it need any more experimentation to know that the dynamics of the observer's consciousness is not separable from the dynamics of the consciousness in the observed object?

Niels Bohr, in his well-known essay entitled "*Biology and Atomic Physics*" speaks of "the impossibility in physical experience to distinguish between the phenomena themselves and their conscious perception (which) clearly demands a renunciation of the simple causal description on the model of classical physics." Can this statement be very far from the mystic's view that subject and object become indistinguishable because one mirrors the other in a self-referent cycle? The mystic has always *known* — he has never felt the need of any confirmation from anyone — that every object is a mirror, that every time one sees an object, one is truly perceiving the subject of that object in its objective manifestation. The usual, ordinary, phenomenal perception can only be a conceptual *interpretation* by an illusory entity that may be called a "psychic complex."

# The Individual Persona

Perhaps the most direct pointer to the real nature of the human being is contained in the oft-repeated story of Chuang Tzu's piglets: the mother sow died while suckling her piglets, and almost at once the little pigs left the dead body because obviously their mother was no longer there. This idea (basic to most religious beliefs) has been prevalent all over the world, though the essential significance was not always grasped. Thus in Europe, the word "animus" was used for that which "animates" the psychosomatic aspect of the sentient beings. However, what was indicated by the word "animus" was different in the West and the East. In the West the word was considered as personal to each individual phenomenal object. In the East the word has had the more comprehensive aspect of "Consciousness" or "Heart" or "Mind" in an impersonal and universal sense.

This impersonal or universal Consciousness, when it manifests itself as the phenomenal universe, objectifies itself as a subject and object. In this process it becomes identified with each sentient object. The result is that the concept of a separate, independent "me" arises in human beings, to whom the phenomenal universe appears to be not just an appearance but a reality with substance, with "thing-ness". This objectivizing of pure subjectivity ("pure" as opposed to the pseudo-subjectivity of the "me"-concept) and calling it "me" as a separate, autonomous entity, is precisely the supposed bondage from which "liberation" is sought.

It is interesting and instructive to go into the process by which the "me" creates a bondage in relation to the Absolute, and how it creates unhappiness and conflict in relation to its relationship with the outside world from which it has separated and alienated itself.

There cannot but be a solution of continuity between an appearance and its source, such as with the appearance of the moon as a reflection in water and the moon itself in the sky. And therefore man has from times immemorial felt an intuitive dissatisfaction with the separation caused by the identification of the impersonal, universal Consciousness with each sentient object. Of course, such separation was basically necessary for the creation of duality. And duality is the very basis of the phenomenal manifestation, of the observer and the observed object, subject and object, pleasure and pain etc. However, man has always been asking himself "who really am I?". He has not, deep down, fully identified himself with the body-mind apparatus. The question itself is at once an indication of his intuitive identification with his source, and an effort to seek that source. In deep sleep there is no separation of any kind. The state of deep sleep is identical for every sentient being. It is a state that every sentient being needs and wants at regular intervals. The condition of deep sleep is a hazy reflection of our real state.

The very first separation occurs when in that primordial state of the Absolute (Consciousness-at-rest), the spontaneous thought "I Am" occurs along with the concurrent appearance of the phenomenal universe as the totality of manifestation. It happens because that is its nature as the totality of potential (the fullness of plenum). The second separation comes about when in its movements as the primal energy — I Am — Consciousness identifies itself with each sentient object, and the "me" concept arises whereby each human being considers itself a separate, autonomous being. This separation is between the "me" and the rest of the world. The rest of the world is then considered as the enemy out to destroy the "me". The "me" strengthens itself by acquiring what it considers as "mine" (relations and friends) thus widening its own sphere. Of course, this circle of "mine" is rather an elastic one, expanding and contracting to drive out those who have turned out to be enemies and to include those who are at the moment considered friends.

The problem for the "me" really is that it knows that the separation is a false phenomenon and that perfection without any boundaries is its true nature. What is not deeply understood is that in this perfection that it seeks, the "me" itself must perish. The "me" is itself the separation that is sought to be corrected. The non-realization of this fact makes the "me" try to improve itself. The unfortunate result of such efforts at self-improvement is that the "me" creates further and deeper separation *within* itself. The deeper this separation goes, the more the confusion arises. The separation between the "me" and the phenomenal world — between the individual organism and the impersonal universal Consciousness — is at a transpersonal level, and therefore at a metaphysical level. However, the further separation caused by self-improvement efforts leads at best to a mental frustration and at worst to total insanity.

The ultimate "happening" of what is generally known as enlightenment, or awakening, or liberation can come about only when there is clear apperception of Reality, the What-Is-Here-and-Now. And the hallmark of this apperception, or ultimate understanding is that it can come about only when the "me" is annihilated. That is to say, it can happen only when the understanding is pure, or without the presence of a comprehender which would put the understanding at an intellectual level. Thus the reading or listening at the transpersonal level is done not with the eye or the ear but with the heart. This puts the "me" further and further into the background until it gets totally annihilated. In the other case, however, the self-improvement efforts are made by the "me", and the more the energy goes into such efforts, the stronger the "me" becomes. What such self-improvement efforts do is to put more and more limitations *within* the "me" concept until the "me" loses all touch not only with the metaphysical Reality but even with the environmental reality — a confusion in the mind leading to insanity.

The creation of limitations *within* the organism proceeds like this. The initial limiting line between "me" and "not-me" is that which separates the organism as such from the rest of the world. That is to say, the boundary line is the skin within which is enclosed the organism. Everything within the skin is "me". Everything without is the "not-me" or the "other", representing the outside world. Within the outside world there is, of course, what is considered as "mine" (the boundary for which is elastic and changes almost continuously depending on the relationships of the "me" with the outside world). However close the "mine" may be, it is still outside the skin-boundary of the "me".

The first schism *within* the organism occurs with the realization that the "me", the ego, while inextricably bound to the body mechanism, is not the body itself. This happens because there is the instinctive feeling that one has a body, that the body is of the nature of a possession, and that the body is more of the nature of "mine" than "me". The basic reason for this schism is ignorance of the fact that the body is indeed of the nature of a possession but that the possessor is not the illusory, conceptual "me" but impersonal Consciousness which has, through identification with the individual organism, lost its universality and has taken on a personal aspect. Indeed, what first considers itself to be in bondage, and then seeks liberation from this bondage, is not the illusory, conceptual "me" but the consciousness itself seeking to shed its personal aspect and return to its impersonal universality.

Actually, the organism is a psychosomatic apparatus which gets its aliveness, its I-am-ness only because it is endowed by Consciousness with its aspect of sentience. In other words, the psyche and the soma, the mind and the body constitute one whole mechanism. The split is not only uncalled for but is indeed the proof of the manner in which the body has been ignored and abused, and the intellect pampered to an extent that the intuitive faculties of the civilized man have atrophied. The result is a lopsided development of the civilized man, leading to tension, conflict and unhappiness. This prejudice in favor of the mind and the schism between mind and body works on the infant, conditioning it continuously. By the time the infant has matured into adolescence, the split is so complete that the individual considers himself primarily the mind. The body is seen as a mere appendage, or as St. Francis referred to his body, "poor borther ass," something to be used to get places in the world. It is because of this dichotomy that there is an inescapable feeling that our decisions and actions are dictated by a tiny man in the head. As soon as there is realization that What-We-Are is the universal Consciousness (which directs all psychosomatic mechanisms like puppets in the play of *maya*) all splits and schisms get healed, and universal harmony prevails.

The immediate result of the body-mind split is that the individual considers himself to be not the total organism but only an aspect of it, that is to say, the mind or the ego. If he is asked, or if he himself thinks, about his identity, he would identify himself with "a more or less accurate mental self-image, along with the intellectual and emotional processes associated with the self-image."

The next step in the process of fragmentation and exclusion within the organism comes about with the limiting of the ego to certain characteristics required by a certain ideal. The ego or the self-image is confined only to an ideal demanded by society and / or commanded by religion. All other characteristics are thrown out of the self-image as part of the not-self. This truncated self-image is what the individual considers to be himself — *the person*.

Thus it is that the conceptual individual narrows himself down until he is totally dominated and bound by *the person*. Duality is the very basis of the phenomenal manifestation in the construct of space-time: space in which objects could be constructed in the three dimensions, and time or duration in which the constructed objects could be observed. All are objects in the manifestation which appears in Consciousness and are observed and cognized by Consciousness in Consciousness. It is only in the duality of the observer-object and observed object that manifestation can function. But as soon as the universal impersonal Consciousness appears as sentience in each object, it identifies itself with each such object in a subject-object relationship, and thereby *apparently* loses its universality and impersonality. The personal or individual consciousness first identifies itself with the individual organism. Thereafter, through intellectual conditioning, it identifies itself not with the whole psychosomatic organism but predominantly with the psyche alone. The body is relegated to the position of the "poor brother ass". Then from the psyche-ego there is a further narrowing down. All the "unwanted" aspects or characteristics of the ego are thrown out and the full self-image of the ego becomes the truncated self-image of the persona. This is the play of *maya* showing the downfall of consciousness first from universality then to the ego and then to the persona. It is like a king dreaming that he is a helpless, destitute beggar.

The significant point in this analysis is that with each narrowing down of identity from universality to persona, the individual creates for himself more and more problems, conflicts and unhappiness. And the tragedy is that he does not realize that *the cause of his unhappiness lies not in the outside world (as he thinks) but within himself.* Thus, the more he tries to protect himself and what he considers as his security, the tighter becomes the bonds with which he has trapped himself. The more efforts he makes with the help of psychologists, psychiatrists, *gurus*, the more trussed he becomes until perhaps a stage is reached when he either commits suicide, or he surrenders to what he considers the inevitable fate.

The fact of the matter is that all efforts must necessarily emanate from the illusory ego — whether full or truncated — which really means from that very mind (thought-intellect) which has brought about such a sorry plight. And the relief, the liberation, is possible only when the mind ceases to function in those areas beyond its allotted routine, technical scope. It comes only when conceptualization ceases. Then the desires, fears, hopes and ambitions go back to their source. This is possible only when there is a total transformation in viewpoint (*metanoesis*). And this can come about only when the mind surrenders itself completely and merges itself in its source, which is Consciousness: I Am. There can be no technique or system for this for the simple reason that all techniques and systems refer to the illusory ego or individual, and for the transformation to *happen*, the ego must vanish. When the mind surrenders, personal consciousness realizes its universality — which is what is really meant by enlightenment. In other words, the true surrender of the mind comports the understanding that the individual (with his truncated aspects) never did exist except as a mere mental construct in Consciousness. It never had any independence or autonomy. And the organism as such is an object like any other in the phenomenal manifestation.

The question that naturally arises at this juncture is: if there is no individual who can make positive efforts, how does the transformation occur? The start of the transformation is a *deep* feeling of utter dissatisfaction with life — what Vedanta calls "dispassion". This feeling is likely to be diagnosed or interpreted by professional people as social maladjustment and given some technical label. Indeed, this is precisely what happened to a Canadian friend of mine. He went from one professional to another, gobbled up medicines literally in dozens, until he suddenly realized that he could not possibly survive another six months at the pace at which he was sliding down into the abyss. He did what very few people would have done. He resigned from a top level executive position, sold his house, handed over all the keys to his nephew, and (after making the necessary arrangements for regular remittances) took the next available plane to India. It so happened that he finally landed at the feet of Nisargadatta Maharaj in Bombay. In the few days before he left Canada for India, friends congratulated him on his bold decision. "I smiled", he told me, "and made suitable noises, but actually I was scared to death, and yet I could not have done otherwise".

This deep sense of dispassion and a sincere dissatisfaction with life is the point of the inward turning of the personal Consciousness. It is the point of no return in the quest for the source. As Ramana Maharshi used to say, once this happens, it is like "putting your head in the tiger's mouth" — the "you", (the "me"), cannot expect to survive. And with the annihilation of the "me" arises spontaneously, naturally, and suddenly the supreme understanding. Dispassion, arising out of the suffering which the persona has brought about, leads to surrender to the What-Is-Here-and-

Now. Past and future cease to have any real meaning because the surrender is to the present moment.

This dispassion towards life, this suffering, must be viewed not as suffering itself but as a symptom of some happening or occurrence as such. When this suffering is taken to be a happening to some "one" (an individual), then what takes place is not really surrender but panic. The two are diametrically opposed. One leads to the breaking of the self-imposed boundaries or limitations which had culminated in the persona, while the other leads to burrowing further down into the narrowed persona, which could lead to tragedy. True surrender presupposes the realization of the helplessness of the individual *because of his illusoriness* (and thus the illusoriness of the boundaries). It therefore leads to liberation from all boundaries.

What is necessary is to prepare a certain ground work for the surrender (the letting-go) to take place. It must be clearly understood that this preparation is *not* positive action — indeed, positive action, like trying to improve oneself by various methods, is what has brought about the persona. The preparation of the ground work is merely the understanding of how the persona boundary (and the other boundaries) has come into being, and how the drawing of a boundary line (any boundary line), means in effect the drawing of a potential battle-line.

What is to be understood is that each boundary means that much limitation in one's self-identity, from no-boundary universality to an inaccurate and emaciated self-image of a persona. The persona boundary gets drawn when there is an absence of recognition that one's phenomenal identity, the ego, is necessarily a mixture. It contains in varying proportions, characteristics and tendencies which are currently considered in terms of good and bad, desirable and undesirable. In trying to improve himself consciously, the individual denies those tendencies which he considers undesirable, and *rejects* them. But such rejected tendencies do not really vanish; they remain and accumulate under the surface. Such suppression is the root cause of many mental disturbances. The realization of the fact that the unwanted aspects of one's ego are an integral part of what makes for a supposed individual is the first step towards relief through surrender.

Once there is a basic realization of — and acceptance of — the oneness of the good and the bad within the individual ego, all that is really needed is letting-go and witnessing of the operation of this realization. It is of the utmost importance to understand that what works is *the impersonal realization in which there is really no comprehender.* As soon as the comprehender intrudes, the surrender is no longer surrender. True surrender implies an understanding and total acceptance of *all* characteristics and tendencies *inherent* in the psychosomatic organism — positive and negative, lovable and despicable — as a part of the totality of What-Is. As this realization becomes stronger and stronger, it continues on its upward course at a faster and faster pace. The illusory individual goes further and further into the background, allowing the harmony of the universality to come to the forefront. In other words, surrender and realization react on each other to partake more vigorously of the current of cosmic energy, so that at some appropriate time what is known as sudden enlightenment might occur. Enlightenment means the healing of the apparent schism between the universal, impersonal Consciousness and the individual personal consciousness.

## The Individual Is The Problem

No animal finds "life" a problem. Man is as much a part of the manifested world as is the animal, and if man finds life a problem, it stands to reason that that problem has been created by himself. To ask whether man should therefore act like an animal is completely to miss the point and pervert the issue.

What the problem indicates (and the problem has intrigued and harassed mankind for ages) is that a comparatively large number of prophets and saints have been laying down rules and regulations (do's and don'ts), for many years, but all to no avail. Indeed, the problem has worsened, both in tension and urgency, so much so that mankind finds itself in danger of annihilation. If one were to suggest that it would not really matter to the totality of manifestation if mankind *did* annihilate itself, he would be considered an insensitive fool. And yet, this is precisely the point. The "problem" is created by man's imperfect perception of the manifested world, and the only way to resolve the problem is not to try to find a solution for it, but to discover why and how the perception is incorrect. If a mirror gives a distorted image, the problem lies not in the distortion of the image but in the defective construction of the mirror. If the perception is corrected, there would be no need of any solution for the problem of life: the problem would just disappear. Very briefly, the imperfection lies in not seeing that the individual who perceives an object and the object itself are not different in essence.

Man has been considering himself as an individual entity entirely separate from the rest of the world. He considers that the rest of the world exists so that he can grab from it anything that he wants for "himself". He extends his hand to the rest of the world not in a spirit of giving his cooperation for mutual benefit but with a view to grabbing whatever he can lay his hands on. Give-and-take for him simply means you give and I take. But the fact of the matter is that no object (and man is very much an object, though of course endowed with sentience and intellect) can exist as an autonomous entity. The individual thinks of himself as a separate being but, as Schopenhauer taught, physical causality is only one of the working principles in the functioning of the world. The other is a metaphysical element, a universal Consciouusness, compared to which personal or individual consciousness is like a "dream compared to reality". In other words, there is an underlying unity in the apparent diversity of the universe. This is the basic principle of all non-dualistic teaching. It is interesting that even in the West, the idea of unity-in-diversity can be traced to the Pythagorean Harmony of the Spheres and the Hippocratic Sympathy of All Things in which, "there is one common flow, one common breathing, all things are in sympathy."

That everything in the universe "hangs together" — partly through apparently mechanical causes but basically through hidden affinities which express themselves as apparent coincidences — has been expressed by many thinkers. According to the considered view of modern physicists, "it is impossible to separate any part of the universe from the rest", and it is interesting to note that as far back as A.D. 1557, Pico della Mirandola summarized the matter succinctly by saying: "Firstly there is the unity in things whereby each thing is at one with itself, consists of itself, and coheres with itself. Secondly, there is the unity whereby one creature is united with the others and all parts of the world constitute one world."

Life becomes a problem for man because he ignores this fundamental fact of unity-in-diversity. The ignoring of this fact cannot but lead to conflict and confusion not only in the individual's relationship with the outside world but also within himself. "At the heart of each of us, whatever our imperfections, there exists a silent pulse of perfect rhythm, a complex of wave forms and resonances which is absolutely unique and individual, and yet which connects us to everything in the universe."

This unity-in-diversity is seen in various phenomena. From the earliest times, there never has been a society of people in which there was no music and dance. Music and rhythm — "the play of patterned frequencies against the matrix of time" — seem to be at the very root of all existence. Surely the intuitive knowledge of this fact is what made Pythagoras say that a stone is frozen music. Modern science now confirms that every particle in the manifested universe draws its natural characteristics from the pitch, pattern and overtones of its particular frequencies. And this seems to apply to all forms and aspects of energy. As one writer has put it, "It is the pulsation, a musical quality called vibrato, that wells up *within* the sounded note that can lead us to what is most spontaneous and creative in human life, and possibly even to deeper mysteries — to powers of knowing and doing which we have lost or given away during the epoch of civilization and which perhaps we may now regain."

It is interesting that the rate of vibration (about seven pulsations a second) of the vibrato precisely matches the *theta*-wave of the brain. The *theta*-wave is associated with the twilight zone between waking and sleeping, in which the divided mind (which normally operates through logic and reason) recedes deep into the background, giving free reign to an expanded consciousness. This expanded consciousness has access to the deepest wells of creation and therefore to extraordinary psychic experiences.

Indeed, a powerful musical vibrato, capturing the rhythm in the brains of the listeners, could quite easily explain the extraordinary effects of Lord Krishna's *bansuri* (wood flute) on the minds of the *Gopis*, wherein all sense of separation could be lost. This would also explain the astonishing effect devotional music has, particularly on certain people whose understanding has greatly developed their receptivity to the vibrato. Actually, the emanation of a single note on a single musical instrument is known to be a matter of incredible complexity: "both volume and pitch interrelate with timbre or tone quality, which is a kind of sum product of all the details through which vibratory energy distributes itself..."

Melody and counterpoint gets created when the single note from a single violin is mingled with notes from other violins and other instruments perhaps in addition to voices, and all these sounds begin to change with time. Indeed if any "problem" is posed in terms of a single part, the solution must lie not in direct relation to the problem but only in terms of "an intricate interwoven complexity of rhythms", that must dissolve the problem itself. In other words, what exists is a single, unified explicit emotion, a "whole" in which *the complexities cannot exist as independent parts.* Indeed, if a note "A" is produced near a violin, the string relevant to the note "A" on the violin will start to vibrate on its own by resonance.

It is not that this phenomenon is confined or restricted only to music. The way music works is not different from the world of objects and events, for the simple reason that everything is truly *vibration* or emanation. Even a quick glance at the yellow wing of the butterfly would make the dye molecules in the retinas of your eyes vibrate, according to scientific calculation, approximately 500 trillion times. If the butterfly happened to be blue or purple, the number of vibrations or waves would increase because that color vibrates faster. The rate of vibration for X-rays instead of light would speed up a thousand times, while in the case of gamma rays, a million times. The vibratory rates of sub-atomic particles making up ordinary matter, we are told, are unimaginably higher while the waves at the heart of the atom's nucleus vibrate at a rate that boggle one's imagination.

It may be that the spiritual Masters gave more prominence to hearing rather than seeing or reading for the simple reason that in the absence of printing — a comparatively recent development — the written word was not easily available. Nonetheless, it is a fact that what connects people more intimately with the matrix of existence is hearing rather than seeing, perhaps because sound seems to have in our life the particularly significant quality "of all-around-ness, of the here-and-now." From this point of view, three phenomena would be of interest:

a) If the rates of vibration of all radiated energy — heat, light, radio waves, X-rays etc. — were arranged in order, the resulting electro-magnetic spectrum would bring out more than seventy octaves, visible light being only one of them. All the "tones" in this spectrum would have their own harmonic overtones with certain similarities appearing at octave levels.

b) There seems to be a reason why many scientists and mathematicians are either musicians themselves or have an active interest in music: the musical nature of the world has been confirmed by many basic scientific discoveries. Thus, the periodic Table of Elements — the list of all chemical elements according to their graded atomic weights — breaks down into seven octaves "with properties that tend to repeat as in musical octaves."

c) W. Ruff, an assistant professor of music and John Rodgers, a professor of geology, in an astonishing experiment, applied the laws and musical notations of Johannes Kepler, the seventeenth century astronomer (who worked out the laws of planetary motion), and came out with startling results. Kepler believed that each of the planets, far from being dead matter, was very much "alive" and that each had its own music. In fact he proceeded to work out each planet's "song" in terms of its orbit around the sun. What Ruff and Rodgers did was to apply Kepler's laws and musical notations to the motion of the planets as projected over a hundred year period starting 31st December 1976. This information was fed into a computer connected to a music synthesizer. What emerged was the music of 100 years of planetary motion, music of the spheres recorded on a thirty-minute tape: "a spectacular if somewhat dizzying piece of music, with Mercury, the fastest moving planet singing the shrill ascending and descending slide of a piccolo, and Jupiter the slowest, sounding a deep, powerful rumble." As professor Rodgers put it, "Venus changes from a major to a minor sixth and earth makes a marvelous minor second. Indeed, the heavens themselves would seem to have been ordered by rhythm, resonance and, above all, harmony."

We are normally accustomed to thinking in terms of action-reaction (stimulus-response) in regard to human behavior. While this may appear to be correct at the superficial level, the fact of the matter is that at the most fundamental level, the listener is not really reacting or responding to the speaker, but in a sense he is *one with* the speaker. The principle behind this seemingly astonishing fact is what is known as entrainment: "Whenever two or more oscillators in the same field are pulsing at *nearly* the same frequency, they tend to 'lock-in' to the same frequency — nature always seeks the most efficient energy level — it takes less energy to pulsate in unison than in opposition." We may not notice it but entrainment exists in all fields of activity, and is an aspect of the compulsive tendency towards perfect rhythm that exists in the very roots of our existence.

Living things contain oscillation. Indeed, although the fact may not be generally realized, living things pulsate or change rhythmically and, therefore, *are* oscillators. In the complex organism of the human being, the frequencies of oscillation constitute a large number and so do the interactions between them. Even the simplest single-celled organism oscillates to a number of different frequencies at various levels, and microscopic examination of these organisms show, we are told, a startling revelation of ceaseless, rhythmic pulsation. What is more, our internal rhythms are entrained not only with one another but also with the total manifestation. Our physical and mental states show noticeable changes in rhythm with the seasonal swing of the earth and Sun, with the tides, with the day-night cycle, and perhaps even with cosmic rhythms that science has yet to isolate and define. When for any reason these rhythms get forced out of phase, disease is not unlikely and dis-ease quite inevitable.

It is because these natural rhythms have indeed been forced out of phase, that man today finds himself confronted with physical disease and mental dis-ease. The consolatory fact is that, in the ultimate analysis, entrainment is not susceptible to long-term manipulation. Since it is the very stuff of life, it must always reflect not only the essential interconnectedness of life and existence, but also the ceaseless change — yet with complete overall balance — that is the basis of the phenomenal manifestation.

Metaphysics has been expounding the oneness and interconnectedness of everything in the universe from times immemorial, but science has accepted the fact only comparatively recently. And one would be considered churlish not to accept it, at least intellectually. The problem of the individual now takes a practical turn: if this is so, why does the individual have problems to face? The answer is that the individual's perception of the world and the objects therein is defective. The basic point about this defective perception is that when a person perceives an object consciously, he is attentive to it as an object. He does not really perceive the object in its totality as the manifestation of the Absolute, representing totality itself. What he perceives is merely an appearance in his mind, based on the response of his sense organs to the contact with this outer object, and relating to the memory of his previous experiences. However, it is a relevant fact that the mental image of the perceived object and the real object are not unconnected. The relationship between the two is comparable to that existing between a sectional plane of a volume and the volume itself. In other words, *the perception is not altogether incorrect, merely inadequate.*

All ornaments made of gold, in spite of wide differences in shapes and sizes, will show the presence of gold (as the basic substance) when tested on a touchstone. Similarly, as everything in phenomenal manifestation owes its relative existence to primal energy, all objects have an inherent aura or vibration or emanation, which is the reflection of the primal energy In other words, there is an identity of structure (in spite of considerable difference in shapes) between all objects. And when one object is perceived by another object gifted with sentience, the emanation from the *perceived* object reacts on the *perceiver*-object's senses which awakens a corresponding complex mental vibration. The mental image thus released in the perceiver is not *produced* by the perceived object but is merely actualized or awakened by it.

If the perceiver-object were *totally* open to the emanation from the *perceived*-object, the communication of the resonance between the two would be at the center of each, that is, at the level of the interconnected identity, at the level of reality. In other words, the perception would be perfect because it would comport the perception of the identity between the perceiv*er* and the perceiv*ed*. The ordinary perception is defective because it lacks the underlying essence or hypostasis of phenomenal manifestation. The "identity-in-the-difference is divided into identity *and* difference". The identity gets displaced by identification. The perceiver forgets his identity with the perceiv*ed*-object as the separate entity and, worse still, forgets the underlying reality in both.

How does the identification come about?  The outer world as the perceiv*ed*-object, offers total resonance through its center.  But the perceiv*er*-object, instead of exhausting the current of resonance (cosmic energy) at its center (in which case the perception would be perfect), allows the current to pass on to the periphery.  Thus the *functional* center gets bypassed and the current moves on the to spurious *operational* center.  The receiving of the current of resonance at the noumenal functional center is perfect perception or enlightenment.  The current passing on to the false operational center means defective perception.  Why should this happen?  Because in the absence of defective perception — which means interpretation of what is perceived — "*maya*" would not be able to function and there would not be any dream-play of phenomenal manifestation that this life presents.

The effect of the defective perception (identification with a mental image), is the creation of a spurious "me" — the supposed "individual" who finds life such a problem. This is because the cosmic flow of energy from the center of the outside world (represented by the perceived object), instead of expending itself in the center of the perceiver-object, passes on to the periphery. Located there is the operational center of the brain-mind which is the seat of the disruptive feeling of acceptance or refusal, and the apparent choice between them. The true significance of this analysis is that while the supposed individual considers the perceived object as the disruptive factor causing the dualistic conflict, the fact is that the conflict is caused by the schism between the true functional center and the spurious operational center within the perceiver-object (the individual).

The essential point to remember is that the conflict is created not by the closing of the true center (which is impossible because that is What-We-Are) but by the superimposition of a closing mechanism on to that open, receiving center. All that is truly needed is to shut off this useless, unnecessary appendage of the peripheral mind of dualism. If the closing mechanism were switched off, the always open functional center of perfect perception would work naturally and spontaneously.

The result of this dualism between subject (perceiver-object) and the perceived-object, between the acceptance of some things offered by the outside world and non-acceptance of others, is a conflict which is generated not by the outside world but *within* the perceiver-object which has assumed volition for itself as a"me". What this means in effect is that the "me" wishes to be non-emotional to unacceptable things while remaining emotional to acceptable things. This apparent conflict can be resolved only by a true understanding of the illusoriness of the "me" and therefore the illusoriness of the conflict. The dilemma is that experiencing means experiencing both joy and suffering, while not-experiencing eliminates the joy with the suffering. This dilemma is fictitious inasmuch as the outside world is not really concerned in it at all. It is all within the "me". The realization of this fact is the true understanding, the illumination, the enlightenment.

The understanding basically is that living includes both joy and sorrow. That all events will take place irrespective of whatever any "me" may want or not want. That total participation — not refusal to the negative aspects of life — is the only answer because the human being is an integral part of the totality of manifestation. The world will go on irrespective of the wants and desires of individual human beings.

This leads to the obvious question: what is to be done to achieve this understanding? Any answer would lead the "individual" to start *doing* something — (meditation or some other "method") — which would be the same as the "doing" of a dog when he is chasing his own tail. This is so because when we pass on to the question "what is to be done", what is forgotten is the basic fact that the one who wants to do something is the illusory "me" and there is no such creature. In fact the whole trouble or conflict and unhappiness and bondage, from which a release is sought, is the creation of the doing by a "me". The "me", by his doing, is constantly creating a spectacle but there is no spectator. To the extent that the "me" sits in meditation and is not experiencing (or doing) anything, he is a spectator without a spectacle. It is only when, as a result of the deep understanding, the "me" remains completely in the background that the "I" (the true nature of man) witnesses the spectacle of nature, the totality of the functioning, and there is both a spectacle and a spectator.

The idea of sitting quietly, neither doing nor not-doing anything, may seem like an invitation for laziness to those who have been taught to be on the go all the time, trying constantly to be on top of the "other" man, straining, viewing, competing against all comers. But this is not so. No one can suppress his inherent nature; the restless man will keep on doing something "positive" while the more cerebral man will sit back and think. But the point is that when understanding is present, neither would think that what goes on is his doing. And the wonderful thing about this ultimate understanding is that it is not to be "acquired" — it cannot be acquired. It cannot be acquired for the simple reason that all of us *are* that understanding. We are not the "individuals" that we think we are.

It is entirely through totally incorrect conditioning, almost from birth, that the individual has reached a point where he thinks that it is the individual with his intellect who makes the world run. In so thinking, man forgets some obvious facts. What makes homing-pigeons return to their roosts after flying long distances? What makes salmon return to the exact spot of their birth to spawn? Indeed, how do the respiratory, circulatory and digestive systems in the human body work without any conscious direction from the brain?!

What human conditioning over thousands of years has achieved is the elevation in status of our brains together with neglect, or even contempt, for our bodies. Through that has come about a sort of dichotomy between the cortex in the brain and the rest of the body. And it is this dissociated brain which is generally referred to as man's will or volition, based on memory. As one writer has put it, "we have allowed brain thinking to develop and dominate our lives out of all proportion to instinctual wisdom which we are allowing to slump into atrophy." The result is that we are at war with ourselves. The brain wants things which the body does not need. The body desires things which the brain does not permit. The brain gives orders which the body cannot follow. And the body creates impulses which the brain cannot understand.

In actual fact, modern life is a vicious circle in almost every respect. The brain resorts to past memories to produce desires which must be satisfied in the future (a condition which is itself an inference). The basic Mind (Consciousness) knows only reality in the present moment whereas the brainy mind — (the divided mind) — lives in the past and the future, and produces more and more desires and hopes and ambitions and frustrations. In other words, our culture has come to mean "an affront to the wisdom of nature and ruinous exploitation of the human organism as a whole."

It is only those who apperceive the utter futility of living in this vicious circle who may be able to take a quantum leap out of it. It is not that the brain is the villain of the piece. The fact of the matter is that the brain, working rightly and naturally, is the highest form of instinctual wisdom. It is verbalizing, wanting to know "how", self-consciousness, which creates the disorder. Understanding produces the effortlessness which makes for harmony. It is the effortlessness — absence of conscious or volitional effort — which makes for understanding. And understanding can *happen* only when there is total absence of any comprehender. In other words, understanding happens only when the comprehender — the individual — merges in the understanding. Then there is only the witnessing of the spectacle or dream of life without the least desire to change anything in the spectacle.

# The Individual's Futile Search For Security

Insecurity has been a problem for the human individual ever since the dawn of time. Aggression from without, and poverty and disease within have been known to many in every age. And even in those rare times when there seemed to be a sense of security, it was only on the surface. For this deep constant sense of insecurity, man could find no answer within. There was nothing which he could control — and therefore he sought refuge in some concept, some myth, some factor that was independent of any change. He created something constant to which he could pray and within which he could seek refuge. He called it God or the immortal soul or Atman or Brahman, or whatever.

The only trouble with any concept such as God or the soul is that it is after all a myth. Often an individual feels this deep within his heart and once the suspicion of the myth is confirmed, its power is gone. A myth can work only so long as a man believes that it is the truth. In the last few years, perhaps a hundred years or so, there appear to be, as one writer says, "fewer and fewer rocks to which we can hold, fewer things which we can regard as absolutely right and true, and fixed for all time." The Newtonian physics, though based firmly on materialism, did not specifically contradict the religious tenets of the universe being ruled and governed by an infallible God by means of eternal laws of right and wrong. All that the man of science could say was that science could not prove whether or not God exists. That is to say, science could not prove that God did not exist, and that was enough for the religious.

What nuclear physics and relativity and the theory of uncertainty have done is to go a vital step further and say that it seems almost certain that the universe was not "created" by any power but that the arising of the universe was a "self-generating process". The confusion is worse confounded by the fact that modern science now views reality not as a conglomerate of separate things with boundaries but as a non-dual network of inseparable patterns, a seamless coat without boundaries or separations. In other words, the individual human today feels utterly lost without his boundaries. He is without the power outside of himself on which he thought he could depend. He is without the strap he could hang on to or the crutch on which he could lean. Actually, what the modern scientist has done is to say that according to his view of the universe, there is hardly any room for meaning, purpose or design by an overall entity with supreme power (by whatever name it might be called). In other words, man is seen as such an integral part of the universe that it seems hardly necessary for a human being to try to divine any specific purpose in life. To say that everything is created and regulated by God is like saying that "everything is round (or rectangular) and is made of such and such materials". It doesn't really tell you anything — it only describes. The effect of this on the common individual, especially in the West, is one of help-lessness, hopelessness and frustration. The result is es-capism through some means or the other — drink, drugs, sex, or even senseless murder and suicide!

But the fact of the matter is that there is a "point of departure". And this point is the frank and open admission that there are really no good reasons for *believing* in any of the common beliefs regarding God, including continuing immortality through the everlasting soul. A firm *acceptance* of this fact (*without any sense of guilt whatsoever*) at once brings about a feeling of total freedom and security. When you give up a *belief*, you give up the sense of insecurity on which that belief was based, and you are free to *know* yourself. Needless to say, such a point of departure is a point of total transformation in one's view of the entire universe, the human individual, the other sentient beings, as well as the insentient part of the universe. There has to be a sense, not of belief, but of faith in the voyage of self-discovery. It is a decision to get out of the existing prison regardless of what the "outside" may hold for us. Our self-dis-covery is now undertaken not with the intention of trying to confirm or find justification for our present preconceived notions and beliefs but with the faith that whatever we find will be the Truth, *the Truth which is self-evident and needs no*

*outside support or justification.* It is with the full understanding that our self-discovery could well be a jump off
the cliff, a plunge into the unknown.

The only thing we *know* for ourselves as a matter of
certainty, without the slightest need of any thought, and
without the need of any confirmation from anyone else, is
the ineluctable fact that each of us can say "I Am". In other
words, I know I exist, I am alive, I am present: I am
conscious. And, what is more, while in deep sleep one is
not conscious of oneself On waking up there is again the
consciousness of being present not only on waking up but
also on having been present during the deep sleep state.
There is an essential difference between the two states of
sleeping and waking: During deep sleep the consciousness
of a "me" as an individual was not there, nor was there any
feeling of insecurity or unhappiness. These arise once
again only on waking up. What it really amounts to is that
what was present in deep sleep is *that Consciousness which
is identical in every individual.* No individual in deep sleep
is concerned with his existence or the awareness of his
existence, either his fears and hopes or his frustrations and
ambitions. These arise only when he wakes up. In other
words, it is the universal or impersonal Consciousness
which is present in the deep sleep state of every individual.
It is only when he wakes up that Consciousness gets tainted
with the individual personality of a "me", with all its fears
and frustrations, hopes and ambitions, joys and miseries.
This should at least make us realize that what we really
need is to stop searching for security, which is a mythical
state of mind. We need to get rid of the tainted "me" which
has transformed universal, impersonal Consciousness into
the personal consciousness of "me". We need to understand the oneness of universal Consciousness in the
astonishing diversity that forms the totality of the
manifested universe. This is the vision of God that all
religions talk about but is clouded by various beliefs and
concepts concerning "God". It is not by striving to escape
from the finite and relative world that we can "attain" the
vision of God. It is only through the *acceptance,* without any

reservation or doubt, of the oneness or identity not only between one manifested object (or individual) and all the others, but also between the manifested known universe and the unmanifest unknown potential, that the true vision of God *happens*.

It is necessary to go to the root of the problem of insecurity in order to really understand it. And in the very understanding of the problem it disintegrates. The sense of security and the feeling of a need for it arises out of a misunderstanding of the basis of what we call life. The fact of the matter is that we do not really see that "change" is an integral aspect of life. What we want is to stop the movie of life at a particular "still", depending upon what that still means to us in terms of what we *then* consider as happiness. When we fail to see *change as life itself*, just as the flow is really the river, we become like Ouroboros, the misguided snake, who tries to eat his own tail. The only way to make sense out of change is to join it. You cannot avoid it! There is no other way. Either plunge into life and welcome change as the spice of life or resist and set yourself against yourself.

The basic question is why is it that man feels insecure with change? Why does this fear of insecurity reach its horror in the concept of death? Essentially it is thought or conceptualization that makes cowards of us, and the base of it is a misconception regarding the phenomenon of "time" or duration. The entire trouble is that we think we are *in* time and that we are subject to the vagaries of time. *But truly we cannot be in time but must necessarily be outside it.* If we were in the flow of the river of time, we could not possibly be aware of the flow. Since we *are* aware of the flow, it must necessarily mean that as the experiencer we must be outside the flow of time. And "outside the flow of time", whether you consider it as a flow from the past to the future or from future to the past, can only mean intemporality. The *only* conclusions, therefore, can be that what flows in the stream of time can only be the phenomenal object, the human psychosomatic apparatus. Therefore, what we truly Are is intemporality, immutability. What this means in effect is that it is only as a phenomenal object that the human individual "flows" from birth to death, from integration to disintegration, from appearance to disappearance. What we truly Are is not phenomena but noumenon.

If this is accepted — that we cannot make sense out of life on the basis of anything fixed — then, life makes sense! Then, we accept that the very basis of life is flux and we get out of the vicious circle of fixity. We get out not by trying to avoid change but by plunging into it, by moving with it, by joining the dance and getting into the spirit of it all without trying to "make sense" out of the purposelessness of the swirling of the dance.

The fact of the matter is that though life is a continuous flow of events, we expect it to "stop" for a while so that we may understand it according to our fixed rules. This attempt to freeze time causes frustration, fear and insecurity. It is this phenomenon that we attempt to explain by the saying "time is the eternal healer."

While we try to study and express the meaning of life in existing fixed terms and labels, many of the terms and labels themselves keep on changing. And where they do not change, they lag behind and simply cannot express the real things which are forever changing both their shapes and contents. In short, while thoughts, words and labels mean separation and isolation like the individual steps in a dance, life actually means change, movement and fluidity like the dance itself.

When man considers himself as a thing (body) separated by a certain amount of skin in space, and limited by birth and death in time, he has in actuality separated himself from the flow of life because of conventional thought. He has forgotten that he is an intimate part of the flow of life expressed in events which cover many supposed individuals. He has forgotten that *the flow of life is irresistible.* In other words, to understand what life is all about, man must first *feel* the conviction that his mind cannot know its own source (the ultimate potential by whatever name called) and that man must give up the feeling of a separate "me" as an autonomous entity, and accept the fact that, as a phenomenal entity, he is subject to the same force or energy that brought him into the flow of life and that will, in course of time, take him out of it. The sense of insecurity disappears when the sense of separation disappears.

The root of the frustration which the civilized man feels today lies in the fact that he lives not for the present moment but for the illusory future, the future which is only a creation of brain and therefore a mere inference based on memory, an abstraction at best. It is the brain, or the divided or split mind, which creates the future whereas the *whole* mind knows no future for the simple reason that it does not conceptualize and lives totally in the present reality. The whole mind knows only "What-Is" whereas the split-mind, working through the brain and its memory, has created a "present future" which has a high degree of accuracy only in so far as the ponderables are concerned. For example, everyone will grow old and will need an income in the absence of the ability to work, everyone will die, etc.. However, the split-mind cannot handle imponderables.

It is clear that the brain, with its fantastic memory bank, is an absolute necessity in order to live in this world. But the trouble is that the individual mind is a split or divided mind and we cannot ignore the whole mind because the whole mind is the *basic* universal Consciousness. Indeed, most physical processes concerning breathing, swallowing, digesting, circulating of blood etc. are extraordinarily complex processes with which the brain has little to do. These processes are called "involuntary" and brushed aside as of little consequence. This is where the root of the whole trouble lies — the dichotomy created in the modern man between his brain (the cortex) and the rest of his body, between the whole mind and the split-mind, between the "I" and "me", between the impersonal or universal Consciousness and the personal consciousness identified with the separate psychosomatic apparatus. In other words, we need both the brain-thinking and the instinctive wisdom to lead a harmonious and well-balanced life, but what we have done is to allow the brain thinking to develop so quickly and so fast that we have almost forgotten all about the instinctive wisdom which has thereby nearly slumped into atrophy. What we have done is to live in the future almost entirely, and have forgotten that it is the present moment which is the reality. The brain also understands that the "future" that it has created is relatively a very short time and that therefore it must cram all possible "happiness" into the present moment. There is thus a vicious circle: the brain, drawing on the memory, sees a future for which it must provide, and, at the same time, knowing that the future is uncertain and extremely limited in duration, it must cram as much as possible into the present moment. The result is a frantic attempt to satisfy, and even compel the senses, to absorb as much enjoyment as possible in the present, while at the same time striving as hard as possible to amass money, which represents the power to command such pleasures in the future: to provide security! It is one mad race against time in which there is no time either to enjoy the present reality or the future illusion — "an affront to the wisdom of nature and a ruinous exploitation of the human organism as a whole".

In saying this, it cannot be forgotten that the brain, with its calculating centers, its memory bank and its reasoning ability, is an indispensable part of the human organism. The point is to not let it run beyond its normal and proper function. Its only function is to serve what is normally regarded as the real and the present, not to allow it to make its flights of fancy, conceptualizing the illusory future. Then Consciousness can at all times be effortlessly witnessing every event and happening in the present moment, be aware of every experience in the present moment.

At this stage of the understanding, the mind begins to ask questions: "I understand the position but what do I actually do about it?" But who asks the question? In deep sleep when the mind was inactive there was neither the problem nor any answer. In fact, the problem was created by the very mind which now seeks an answer to the problem. If this is seen in the most vivid way — if one is consciously and wholly aware of the reality of the present moment without any concepts or judgement — it will also be seen that the only thing to do is to remove the unnecessary conceptual matter which prevents the seeing of the truth. What is the truth? The truth is that it is futile to seek perfect security in a world whose very nature is changefulness, fickleness and fluidity! Indeed, such seeking in fact means wanting to be separate from the real world of flux, and it is this very separation which makes for the dreaded insecurity. One nation arms itself in order to achieve security and finds instant retaliation. Any action other than the deepest awareness of the situation can only be counter productive. The crux of the matter is to apperceive that the very concept of security is illusory. There is no such thing as security in this world, not even the security that we will be able to take our next breath!

There is the Sufi story of the sage who, in answer to his knock on the door of Heaven, was asked "Who is there?" and the sage answered, giving his name and saying "It is I". The voice replied, "In this house, there is no room for thee and me". The door remained closed After many years of meditation on this happening, the sage came a second time and the whole process repeated. Then again after further long meditation, the sage realized the truth, and when he called the third time, his answer to the question, "Who is there?", was, "It is thyself" and the door was opened. The sage had then indeed become God.

A similar story concerns Lao Tzu and one of his disciples. The disciple came to Lao Tzu with his face radiant, and said, "Master, I have arrived." The Master was sad but firmly denied that the disciple "had arrived". The disciple went away disappointed. He returned after a few months again, his face full of peace and contentment. He told the Master, "*It* has arrived." The Master looked at him and warmly embraced him.

The point is that the true understanding goes far deeper than an intellectual agreement. The understanding or conviction must reach a depth where the seeker of the security — the individual "me" as a separate entity — has disappeared. The understanding to be effective must stand on its own without the crutch of a "me". Such understanding can come only through constant and continuous awareness of our experience of the present moment — our thought, our desire, our feeling, our sensation — without prejudice, without memory, without judgement. The ordinary normal experience, whatever it may be, disappears together with the disappearance of the moment in which it occurred but leaves a memory of it in the brain. In the experience *as such* there is truly no experiencer — no "me" — that depends wholly on the memory for its illusory existence. In other words, such an experience leaves no psychological scars.

It is of the utmost importance to avoid letting the mind — the "me", the ego — take over at this stage and try to obfuscate the true understanding by all kinds of questions at an intellectual level. It is of the utmost importance to realize that the "me", as a separate experiencer or thinker, is an illusion. It is the illusion which seeks security. To apperceive this fact — to accept this fact with unshakable faith (not merely intellectual belief) — is to see in the plainest possible manner that life can only be experienced in each present moment and that therefore in life there can be neither security nor permanence. To understand each present moment means to remain undivided from it (to be fully aware of it). It means realizing that in each present moment there is eternity, that *it is only intemporality that can be aware of each moment in temporality.*

What happens in moments of sheer joy or pleasure? We have no difficulty in *being* the experience of the moment by forgetting "ourselves" (the "me" is absent and there is only the joy of the experience). The mind remains whole and is not divided from the experience. The problem arises only when there is pain whether actual or imagined, and then the vicious circle of the split mind begins its course, with the effort of the "me" to escape from the pain and the consequent tension. A conscious relaxation of the entire body-mind releases the tension — and the pain — to an astonishing extent. This conscious relaxation is the outcome of the awareness of the fear itself, together with the realization that tension can only make the pain worse. The fear is really based on *the memory* of past experiences and not on the past experiences themselves because those are dead. The relaxation is an expression of the willingness to welcome the new experience without any mental resistance or reservation.

The relaxed acceptance of each new experience means in effect being totally sensitive to each new moment, with a whole, receptive mind. It is important and essential to bear in mind that this is not a pretty theory but an actual fact, open to experiencing. The unrestrained, relaxed receptivity to the ever fresh new moment summons from the depths of one's beingness, unused, natural reserves of power to absorb pain and relieve insecurity. This fact can be witnessed in many aspects of actual life: the "new" importance given to the natural system of giving birth; the very basics of *judo* and *aikido*; floating as against swimming against the current; the comparatively recent principle of providing "give" in a building to withstand storms or earthquakes, etc. Next time you are in the dentist's chair and he picks up his drill, consciously note how horribly tense your body is. Then, consciously relax the whole body and you will find that your mind has also relaxed and is receptive to the next moment, and that the actual pain is *considerably* less than what was conceptualized by the mind. What all this really means is that you will try to escape from pain or insecurity only so long as the "me" keeps itself separate from the experience. When the separation is healed by the realization that the pain is an inescapable experience, the brain experiences the pain in the same total "unselfconscious" way as it experiences joy. The pain as such cannot be escaped — the greater pain is the effort to get away from it. It is vital to realize that this is not a kind of trick to be used on special occasions; it is the very way of life. Always be alert and sensitive to the present moment which truly is never a new moment but one which is ever present as eternity.

It should thus be clear that, as Nisargadatta Maharaj never tired of repeating, "Understanding is all." There is no question of altering or amending the "What Is." The

What-Is is merely to be seen with clarity, with alertness, without the obfuscation of thought and conceptualization. Therefore, the very question of any method or technique is totally irrelevant. The Master can only say, "Open the window— there is the view." The question of how to see the view does not arise.

Thought, words, logic and reasoning are obviously necessary to lead a normal life but they do not constitute "living" by themselves. They are all based on memory of the known and are products of the split-mind (the mind divided by the intrusion of a "me"). To live, whenever possible, without thought, without words, is to be receptive to the unknown with the whole mind. Both are necessary but conditioning over a long period has brought man to the point where to recede into the whole mind is considered being lazy, a waste of one's time! Men of genius, who have been the achievers in the world, have openly admitted that their most revolutionary ideas and inventions have "oc-curred" only when conscious thinking had ceased and the mind was therefore receptive to the unknown.

The significant point, however, is that this suspension of thought — which is in fact the surrender of the split-mind of the illusory "me" — is not restricted to the great achievers of the world. It is possible for every human being who is prepared to see the What-Is with an open mind without resorting to the dead past collected in memory. It is possible if one is prepared to accept life as a reality to be experienced in the present moment and not as a problem to be solved at an intellectual level. In other words, although it may not be given to many to be prophets, it is certainly given to quite a few of us to see the What-Is with clarity of the mind and be enlightened sages. It should not be too difficult, given the necessary sincerity and determination, for an average person to understand life in a sense larger than the view of a split-mind "me". We all experience (at least occasionally) the ultimate Reality. This is possible, of course, only when the seeking is not based on the unreality of the known, pursued through the illusory "me" as a separate entity. Reality is not a discovery which will merely confirm what is already known; it *is* the vast unknown from which has arisen the little that is known to us.

Where have we arrived at this stage? We have come to realize that we do not really know what we want. Our wants are no longer our basic needs, they have become our requirements. What is more, our requirements have become contradictory in the sense that we want to have our cake and eat it. We want security for the "me", which at once means keeping the "other" out of my domain, for the "other" has become an enemy. And yet we also want, at the same time, brotherhood and universality! We want peace and prepare for war. Realization of this fact has also made us realize that problems arise and cannot cease if we look outward from the viewpoint of the individual (whether as a person or a community or a nation) and that our split-vision of the divided mind can heal only if we look at What-Is from the viewpoint of Totality.

The healing of the split-mind into the viewpoint of Totality necessarily means a radical transformation of our view of the world, a *subjective* experience of the organic unity in the world. This subjective feeling of "I" as the center of the universe can *arise* only when the objective illusion of the "me" against the "other" has totally disappeared. And the only way this can happen is when there is total acceptance of the ineluctable fact that I am *not* the master of my fate, nor am I the captain of my soul, that the "me" as a body is a mere object, like any other object in the manifestation, though it is injected with sentience and intellect. Man has no control of his birth, nor of his death, nor of the in between. The only surrender that can take place is to accept this fact and let go! Then one carries on in life allowing one's natural talent to work its own way without the aggressive intent to "make things work".

Whenever there is the subjective experience of the "I"-feeling, there is necessarily the absence of the "me" feeling of being separate, of being isolated, of being insecure. In the beginning a certain amount of patience is necessary to sit quietly (without any specific purpose) and let the "me" get into the background along with the thought process based on it. But when it happens, the inner experience of unity with one's surroundings comes floating in. One must be clearly aware of the fact that the inner experience of unity is on quite a different level from the purely sentimental feeling of the poet for nature, which is entirely superficial. The true oneness includes the realization that it absorbs the bad and the creepy along with the good and the benign. The subjective experience of unity is not a "feeling" which bursts out into song, nor is it an unusual state of mind like a trance (hypnotic or otherwise). It is an intensely deep experience defying verbal expression, indeed it is quite impervious both to description and logic. As a Chinese Master put it, "When you want to see into it, see into it directly. When you begin to think about it, you have missed it altogether." And when you have thus seen it, there is no need to tell the countryside about it from the housetop. It is enough to *know* that you are all that you see and all that you do not see.

It is a traumatic experience — the transformation of one's being — to deeply realize that you really cannot be separate from the universe because what one calls "me" (illusory or otherwise) and the thoughts produced in that "me " are all intrinsic to What-Is. How then can one be separate? How then can one ever have any "security"? Any feeling of security must necessarily be a transient, illusory movement in the mind. Once there is the apperception of this indubitable fact, there *happens* the sort of "letting go," which the average man just cannot understand or even conceive, because by trying to stand outside himself, that is, outside his sensations and emotions, desires and feelings, he has become an enormously confused entity, for whom life is nothing but continuous tension, frustration, conflict and disillusionment.

When there is apperception of the totality of What-Is, the meaning of life becomes very clear: life is just a dance, the purpose and meaning of which is only to dance, and when the dance is over, you are precisely where you were — on the floor. When you dance, there is no expectation of anything to achieve. Before you started to dance, you were still and then there was movement when the dance began, and when the dance ended, there was again stillness. You were born and the movement began; when you are dead, the movement will have ceased and "you" will be back in that state of rest which existed before you were born. It is the sense of "me" expecting, thinking, desiring, hoping, fearing, which deprives life of its meaning and gives death the significance which it really does not have. To the whole mind, death is the unknown potential from which has arisen the birth and the life. To the whole mind death is just another moment in life, complete in itself and unknown until it arrives.

# BOOK FOUR

*Ultimate Understanding Is Itself The Solution*
*—The Final Truth—*

# How To Live One's Life

How to live one's life is really a misconceived problem. It presupposes that one is an autonomous entity with independence of choice and action and that it is possible for one to live according to one's own sweet will and pleasure, depending on one's intentions and aims.

Only a little thought and an honest analysis of the events in one's own life will clearly show that as an apparent entity man does not live his life but that he is *being lived* like a puppet. The attempt by a lived puppet to live what he mistakenly considers his own life is not essentially different from the attempt by a dreamed puppet to live his own life in a dream. The pertinent point is that for both (the lived puppet and the dreamed puppet) the attempts are the only "reality" they could possibly know, whereas in fact both are puppets and their attempts to live their lives are nothing more than reactions to impulses engendered by psycho-physical conditions over which they have no control. Such conditions may be either inherent to the psychosomatic apparatus or environmental or social or habitual, but the fact remains that the reactions to these conditions are what are considered "living one's life". The basic fact is that both the lived puppet and the dreamed puppet are essentially their sentiency — and not the physical form — and the sentiency of both is nothing but a reflex of the mind, a movement in Consciousness which is all that they are.

It is the "me"-notion that is supposed to have volition and which believes that it is leading its own life. And the "me"-notion itself is merely a movement in Consciousness, and therefore all its supposed acts of volition are nothing more than a fantasy. The absence of the fantasy of dreaming denotes the bliss of deep sleep. And the absence of the fantasy of living denotes the bliss of the awakened or enlightened life.

What does this mean in the final analysis? It means that volition is not at all an effective element in phenomenal life because there is no entity as such to have any effective volition. It means further that an apparent act of volition can only mean an ineffective and vain gesture when in accord with the inevitable, and can resemble only the frustrated fluttering of a caged bird when in disaccord.

It is for this reason that Nisargadatta Maharaj used to say "Understanding is all." True understanding comports the abandonment of all volitional activity and therefore actually means *letting ourselves be lived*, because then there is neither volition nor volitional non-volition (deliberately inhibiting volition). The abandoning of volition is brought about by the understanding itself and is not a deliberate act of volition. The consequent absence of ego-activity leaves the mind open for direct or intuitional apprehension so that the mind can function as whole-mind without the conceptual working of the split-mind of dualism.

Such intuitive non-volitional "being lived" is noumenal living that knows not the suffering which is the dubious prerogative of the conceptual entity.

# The Essence Of The Teaching

The essence of the teaching of non-duality is contained in the assertion that there is a single immanent reality which is at once the source, the substratum and the true nature of everything that is manifested as the universe. This reality is directly experienced by every human being, indeed by every sentient being. Different names are given to this one reality, depending on the aspect that is referred to.

Perhaps the most common term by which this indivisible reality is known, is Self, the pure being, a subjective awareness of I Am, the sense of presence as such (not the sense of individual presence) without any subject-object relationship. There is only an awareness of *being*, a consciousness of existing and being present — and this is common to every sentient being. The direct experience of this Consciousness comes about *when the limitations of body-mind separateness are absent*. This direct experience is what is traditionally known as *Sat-chit-ananda* (being-consciousness-bliss). The state of deep sleep, which every human being craves after being awake for a certain length of time, is but a pale reflection of this unbroken bliss because the deep sleep state alternates with the waking state and is therefore not unbroken. The beingness, the consciousness and the unbroken bliss are really not three separate attributes of the Self; they are one unitary experience. They are three notional aspects, much like the three inseparable properties of water: wetness, liquidity and transparency.

The Self is eternally present and always experienceable. Indeed, all there is, is the Self. But the awareness of it comes about only when the self-limiting tendencies of the mind, the conceptualizing and the objectivizing, are not in operation. When these tendencies have totally ceased, the full light of the Self shines forth in all its glory. This state is what is known as Self-realization.

The aspect of the Self, the power or energy that maintains the universe, is what is generally understood by the term "God", or "Shiva", or various other terms in the many religions, including the term "Brahman" used in Vedanta. In the teaching of non-duality, God is not a personal entity, the creator of the universe. The manifested universe is a mere emanation from the unmanifest Source. The Self or Consciousness is immanent in the manifestation because without it, the universe has no independent existence. At the same time, Consciousness-at-rest (or the Self) is not affected by either the appearance or the disappearance of the universe through the movement in Consciousness, and it therefore transcends such manifestation.

The direct experience of the Self is known as *jnana* or Self-realization. There is often an avoidable misunderstanding because the term *jnana* is taken to mean that there is a *separate* individual who has knowledge of the Self. It is astonishing how persistent this misunderstanding remains. Unless care is taken to understand the term *jnana* in its full significance, the spiritual aspirant will base his quest on a totally erroneous belief. The state of Self-awareness cannot come about unless the notion of a separate individual has been totally erased. In the state of Self-awareness there cannot exist any particular individual knower of the Self. *Jnana* is a direct, subjective awareness of the one indivisible reality in which *jnana* is not an object of understanding or experiencing, and in which the subject-object relationship has ceased to exist. In fact, although the term *"jnani"* is used for the purpose of communication, to denote "one" who is firmly established in the state of Self-awareness, it must be clearly understood that the term *"jnani"* is in reality a misnomer inasmuch as the jnani is not to be taken as a separate individual.

Spiritual aspirants are notionally divided into three classes according to their capacity to receive and apprehend the teaching of non-duality:

    (a) those in such an advanced spiritual state (the evolution having perhaps been spread over many "lives", though there is no question of any particular entity going through the evolution, because the "entity" is nothing but an illusory notion) that the apperception takes place as soon as the *guru* explains the true nature of the notional individual in the notional universe;

(b) in the second category those that need to put in some efforts to understand the teaching in its full significance before Self-awareness can take place;

(c) those in the third category need many years of spiritual instruction of one kind or another before they are ready for the final step. Ramana Maharshi used the simile of combustion to describe the three spiritual levels. A single spark is sufficient to ignite gunpowder, while a minimum amount of heat is needed for charcoal, and a considerable amount of work by way of drying and heating would be necessary before wet coal could start burning.

For those aspirants at the higher spiritual level, it is sufficient for the *guru* to explain that the Self alone exists, here and now, all the time. All that is necessary for the Self to be experienced is for the notion of the not-Self, the illusory individual entity which acts like an eclipse on the Self, to be erased. As soon as this primary misconception of the identity with the body is lost, the entire mass of the wrong notions obscuring the light of the Self vanishes, and then there is nothing to interfere with the continuous, unbroken awareness of the Self. At this higher level, as the ground has been already prepared, the question of conscious effort cannot arise. As Nisargadatta Maharaj used to say, all that is needed is the understanding that there is truly no "one" to achieve anything like enlightenment. All there is is the eternal Self, and all that is necessary is the unbroken awareness of that Self. And, what is most important, this awareness, which already exists, here and now, is most natural and spontaneous. There is no question of any effort because there is no "one" to make any effort.

While there are few spiritual aspirants at any one time ready to receive the *guru*'s instruction like a spark for gunpowder, there is a very large number of aspirants who are like wet coal and would therefore need considerable preliminary preparation to purify the mind in order to be able to receive *any* spiritual instruction. For this latter type on the lowest level, Nisargadatta Maharaj would recommend listening to spiritual singing (*bhajan*), counting beads and repeating His name, etc. In between these two extreme levels is the class of aspirants who are neither the spiritual gunpowder nor the wet coal. These belong to the dry charcoal category who need a certain amount of discipline, a certain amount of spiritual heat to be prepared before the combustion can take place. It is for this middle class that the practice of Self-enquiry is prescribed. The aim of Self-enquiry is to discover by direct experience — not merely at the intellectual level — that there is no such thing as a mind. The discovery relates to the fact that every conscious activity — whether of the body or of the mind — is inevitably based on the existence of the "me" concept. It is further discovered, again by direct experience, that the "me" is not an independent or autonomous entity but merely a mental modification, an illusory reflection of the Self. Through the continuous and ceaseless use of Self-enquiry (which need not interfere with the work of daily life), the "me" concept disappears along with all the conceptualization based on it. And when this unnecessary obstruction is removed, Self-realization *happens*. In this state of enlightenment, there exists no individual thinker, no individual observer, no individual do-er, — indeed no "individual" at all. All there is is the sense of presence *as such* — I Am. The absence of "me" is the presence of "I".

It is of utmost importance to understand the significance of this classification. The very basis of the teaching is that there is no such thing as an independent individual entity and that the supposed individual is merely a concept, a mental modification, an illusion. If this is clearly understood and accepted with deep conviction, it would naturally follow that enlightenment is merely a phenomenon, a happening that occurs as part of the totality of functioning in the universal play. It happens through the instrumentation of a particular body-mind mechanism. The appropriate body-mind apparatus that presents itself at the appropriate time and place is also part of that happening named enlightenment. This can be apperceived only when the whole process of evolution, culminating in the *appropriate situation of enlightenment*, is viewed in an impersonal manner. There cannot be identification with any particular aspirant in any class, either with satisfaction at being in a higher class or with disappointment at being in a lower one. And the real joke is that such impersonal viewing (perspective) is itself part of the totality of functioning: it does not happen until the "proper" time! Such impersonal understanding does not happen except at a certain higher level, and such higher level cannot be reached unless there is such understanding!! This *apparent* conundrum resolves itself when it is kept in mind that all conundrums, all riddles, all apparent contradictions exist only in the split-mind based on subject-object relationship. They resolve themselves as soon as they are viewed from the viewpoint of Totality. Totality *is* when the illusory separate individual entity *is not*. When the individual "me" is absent, there can be no desire to change from "What-Is" to "what-should-be" (from the individual's viewpoint). At whatever level a body-mind apparatus may be in the evolutionary scale, there is no question of satisfaction or dissatisfaction in the witnessing of the subjective "I".

This most important aspect of the matter is often overlooked by the spiritual teacher who in his very exegesis unfortunately praises the "one" at the higher level and, directly or indirectly, sneers at the "one" at the lower level. He compares the aspirant at the top to a racehorse who puts in his best as soon as he sees the whip, whereas the aspirant at the lowest level will not be able to grasp the teaching "even if Shiva becomes his *guru*", because he is like the horse who will not run even if he is whipped. Such a simile can only serve to strengthen the ego, the "me" concept. It has happened, as part of the totality, that different aspirants exist at different levels *in accordance with the Grand Design*. There is no question of credit or guilt, success or failure, as an individual. The individual entity is an illusion. Of course, everything is a part of the totality of functioning within the Self. Both the *guru* and the disciple are a part of the totality. And the totality of functioning is itself a dream within the Consciousness. The fundamental truth is that nothing has really happened. There is no creation, no destruction; neither free will nor predestination; neither path nor goal.

The primary and basic source of the "me" concept is identification with an object. The "me" does not exist independently of the object with which it is identified. It is the "me" which claims the association with all thoughts. If there is no thought, there is no "me"; and if there is no "me", there is no thought, no desire. The apparent continuity of the "me" is entirely because there is incessant conceptualizing, unceasing objectivizing — all based on desire in one form or another. All there is is the Self. The supervening "me", and its desires and thoughts, prevent the communion with the Self because this illusory "me" assumes the subjectivity of the "I". The whole purpose and aim of Self-enquiry is to *focus the attention intensively and ceaselessly on the "I" so that the imposter "me" and his identifications are exposed*. "To whom does this desire or thought occur?" is the incessant spotlight which relentlessly exposes the "me". The point is that the "me" concept itself — like all concepts — can only arise from the Self and, if not pursued, will subside back into the Self. Continuous awareness of the falsity of the "me", and its thoughts and desires, focuses the attention on the source of all thoughts and desires and concepts — the I Am awareness of subjectivity, or Consciousness.

It is of primary importance to note that the final demolition of the "me" does not come about by being aware of, or conscious of the subjective "I" because it can only be the furtive "me" who, as the pseudo-subject, is conscious of the object "I". The "me" can never be the subject and "I" can never be the object. It is only by *being* the subject "I", and by *being* the subjective awareness I Am, that the "me" gets annihilated. Any method that does not take into account this basic element cannot be finally effective because any method that expects the "me" to undertake the relevant *sadhana* (spiritual exercises) will only strengthen the "me" concept instead of eliminating it. Such methods will, of course, have certain results like quieting of the mind or the production of certain blissful experiences. But such experiences themselves hold the inherent hazard of being mistaken for the ultimate realization.

Once it is realized that every human being is, at any time, a point in the evolutionary graph line, it is simple to understand not only the existence of the various forms of spiritual teaching but the suitability of each for some people who are at a particular point. The saint says, "do not bother about anything else, just keep repeating the God's name whenever you find the time". Someone else says, "a visit regularly once a week to the church or the temple or whatever is enough". Patanjali says, "make efforts (*Yama, Niyama*) and achieve *Pranayama, Pratyahara, Asana* — it may take time, it may take births, but Hatha-Yoga will get you there." And so on. Each has its place in the spiritual evolutionary scale.

It would be difficult to find anything more direct, more confident (of course, only for those who happen to have the requisite capacity) spiritual instruction than that given by the Sage Ashtavakra to his royal disciple, King Janaka:

*"You are neither earth nor any of the other elements. You are the Self which is the witness of all these, the universal Consciousness.*

*If you dis-identify yourself from the body and remain in Consciousness — I Am — you will be free from bondage here and now, this instant.*

*You are neither of Brahmana nor of any other caste. You are not perceivable by the senses. Be happy in the knowledge that, unattached and formless, you are the witness of everything.*

*Virtue and vice, pleasure and pain (and all other interrelated opposites) are of the mind. Being neither the doer nor the sufferer, you are for ever free.*

*This alone is your bondage, that you see yourself not as the witness that you truly are, but as something else.*

*You are the Consciousness-bliss in and upon which appears superimposed this apparent universe.*

*You are immanent in this apparent universe and this universe has no other existence. Your very nature is pure Consciousness. Do not let your petty mind convince you otherwise."*

For those who find this most direct approach difficult, the usual prescribed method is Self-enquiry, the basis of which is the focussing of attention on the inner feeling of "I" (not "me"), the sense of impersonal presence. In the early stages, the practice of Self-enquiry is necessarily an intellectual activity, but soon the intellectual perception of the "I" gives place to a subjective experience which is totally dis-identified from objects and relative thoughts. The final stage of Self-enquiry is reached when an effortless awareness of I Am prevails, though not incessantly. Self-realization is when this effortless awareness is incessant, but the important point is that this state cannot be "achieved" for the simple reason that the "me" who is supposed to make the effort is on his way to annihilation.

And this state of Self-realization is invariably sudden, though not necessarily a violent phenomenon. Possibly the clearest indication of it is the *total* absence of any doubt: any doubt or problem can exist only at the personal, individual level, never at the level of Totality. When there is no doubt, there is no question of any guilt-feeling — whatever happens is part of the functioning of Totality.

The essential significance of the continuous awareness of the I Am is, contrary to the general belief, that it prevails irrespective of what one is doing. This is so because such awareness means mere witnessing (without involvement) of whatever goes on. It goes without saying that in such a state of awareness or witnessing, the practice of regular periods of meditation is irrelevant.

The practice of Self-enquiry or awareness or witnessing is a gentle, negative technique — if at all it can be so called — to get rid of the positive conditioning that has accumulated over a long period, and is totally different from the usually oppressive and repressive methods of controlling the mind. Curiously near to it is the method of surrender to God as a means of achieving Self-realization, or more accurately, liberation from bondage. The path of surrender is generally associated with *bhakti* (devotional practice) which is essentially dualistic in nature. The point that is often missed or ignored in such devotional practices is that the "me" concept (illusory individual entity) gets stronger and stronger. The separation between the individual and his "God" gets wider and wider, if there is a motive or purpose or a desire to be satisfied, behind the devotional practices. *Even the desire for liberation or enlightenment will make the surrender incomplete* or partial because the supposed individual makes an effort to get or achieve something in return. It is then only a business transaction; there is desire behind the efforts.

The only true surrender is when there is no "one" to ask questions or to expect anything. This means surrendering the *total* responsibility for one's life, for all one's thoughts and actions, to a higher power, God, or Self. Obviously, such self-surrender presupposes that one can not have any will or desire of one's own — which means in effect the acceptance of the fact that there is no individual entity with ability to act independently of God. This actually amounts to a constant awareness that it is only the Self that prevails and that the supposed individual is truly an irrelevance in the totality of functioning. In other words, there is really no significant difference between Self-enquiry and surrender because in both, the "me" is finally to be isolated and annihilated.

# The Basis Of Self-Enquiry

Self-enquiry means enquiry into:
    (a) the nature of the Self,
    (b) the nature of the world,
    (c) the nature of Truth.
Enquire into the nature of Truth thus:

> *You are ever free, why do you call yourself bound and then seek liberation? As the absolute noumenon, you are infinite — how and by whom could you be bound? You are not confined to the body. Whether the body is dead or alive, is truly of no concern to you. The relation between the body and you is like that of the cloud and the wind, or of the lotus and the bee. The wind becomes one with space when the cloud disappears; the bee flies into space when the lotus withers. Death does not affect you who are Consciousness itself. It is your identification with the body as a separate entity which is the cause of your misery.*

Enquiry into the nature of the Self dispels this mistaken identity, and the very dispassion that starts this enquiry is sufficient to bring about the annihilation of that illusory entity, which has no independent nature of its own

The instruction from the *guru* needs to be contemplated seriously:

> *I am surely not this outside world which I can perceive as an inert thing. Nor am I the body created out of a single sperm cell, which seems to "live" for the briefest of moments in the river of time. I am thus not the form, nor the name which is only a sound, a movement in air devoid of any independent existence. Nor could I possibly be the experience of any other sense like touch, taste, or sight or smell. What remains then? — peace*

*beyond any thought! I can only Be that peace which is beyond all concepts and conceptualization.*

It is as if a sudden recollection has dawned:

*I am the Self, omnipresent, the very source of all thought and experience, the inner light of Consciousness because of which the entire manifestation arises and becomes perceivable and cognizable.*

*I am this Self, the experiencing, the Sole experiencer of everything, with a thousand hands and a thousand eyes.*

*This universe exists in me, the infinite Consciousness, like a reflection in a mirror. As the basic energy of Consciousness I exist in all things that exist, as their very essence. I am the fragrance in flowers, the sentience in sentient beings. I am the noumenal transcendence and the phenomenal immanence in the entire manifestation.*

*I am Consciousness without the slightest touch of objectivity or the slightest taint of any modification. What a joke! I who have never been bound, seek liberation! There is neither bondage nor liberation. There is nothing for me to acquire or to abandon. For me who has neither happiness nor misery, where is the question of meditation or non-meditation? There is nothing that I should do or not do. Let the spontaneous action take place, whatever it be. I am the Witnessing of it.*

The notion of the existence of the universe can arise only when the spirit of Self-enquiry is absent. "I" being present before the universe could ever appear, no notion about the universe and anything or anyone therein could possibly concern this "I" that I am (and each of us truly is). Whatever I may be engaged in doing in this life, I cannot be disturbed by any happening because I am beyond all duality and non-duality, as in deep sleep. It is as if I am in deep sleep although actively engaged in life.

In the peace and quietude of one's own inner being, the mystical vision of the universe appears, owing to the vibration of the Consciousness. In the absence of the movement or vibration of the Consciousness — when consciousness is at rest or in a state of abeyance as in deep sleep or under sedation — the universe cannot appear. In this appearance of the universe in Consciousness, there is nothing other than Consciousness. Nothing has any substance of its own — neither the world, nor the sentient and insentient beings, neither the *guru* nor the disciple nor the instruction!

Movements in Consciousness constitute the mind. The realization of this basic fact means cessation of thought and conceptualizing. It means liberation from the bondage of the mind and the ego. Non-realization of this fact means the vicious circle of ignorance and mental activity, each strengthening the other in ever-increasing intensity. The essential point to understand is that any movement in consciousness creates thought and desire, and such movement does not distinguish between desires. These qualities are irrelevant and immaterial. Every thought based on the ego means desire, and desire strengthens further thought. The deep significance of this fact is two fold:

(a) apperception brings about the cessation of desire, positive or negative — that is to say, the cessation of the desire to accept and the cessation of the desire to reject — the desire to accept the acceptable and the desire to reject the unacceptable; the desire to accept what people will applaud and the desire to reject what people might condemn. When there is apperception, there is the clear understanding that *it is the energy of the Consciousness which experiences all experience;*

(b) all desire means movement in consciousness, which is conceptualizing and therefore bondage. Desire includes even the desire for liberation! This is so because it can only be the ego which desires anything, including liberation. Awareness and apperception of this fact destroys the ego, and then enlightenment is apperceived as not a personal event but a happening in totality. Who is bound by whom — and who is liberated by whom?!

True happiness cannot arise until the identification with the body-mind apparatus is demolished. The mind recognizes its own illusoriness when it perceives the body as distinct from itself and abandons its own conditioning in the form of various concepts. Mind and body are each other's enemies and there is suffering when they confront each other in mutual conflict.

Consciousness gives birth, through its own cosmic energy, to the body and the mind feeds the body continually with its own sorrow generated by various concepts. On this basis the dualism of friend and foe is created. Whatever gives pleasure is a friend and whatever gives pain is a foe.

The body in its own intelligence realizes that it is the mind which creates suffering and unhappiness for it, and makes continuous effort to get away from the mind. Both get tired of this constant conflict and succeed in getting away from each other during deep sleep when consciousness is absent. But such absence of consciousness as in deep sleep or under sedation is only temporary. Both body and mind continue to live and function together in the role of the illusory individual entity.

When death occurs, the body dies but the mental conditioning in the form of thoughts, desires, ambitions, etc. remains in the totality of the Mind in Consciousness. At a point in the evolution of the total functioning, it will be the cause of another psychosomatic mechanism which will be created in due course. If, however, conceptualization ceases altogether and there is apperception of "What-Is", the existence of the physical body is of no relevance. At that point, no relationship exists between mind, body and senses. The psycho-somatic mechanism then exists for the balance of its life as a part of the totality of the functioning without any illusion of volition.

When the mind has become vacant through the total absence of all concepts concerning phenomenal existence, what remains is pure Consciousness without any personal identification or notions of objectivity This is the state brought about by the apperception of "What-Is".

This is what is achieved by Self-enquiry. It is not merely a matter of repeating "Who am I?" like a *mantra*, in which case it would not have much value. The aim of Self-enquiry is to focus the mind at its source to the exclusion of all thoughts and concepts. It is not at all a matter of the "me" searching for the "I", or the "I" searching for the "me". In one case the thief himself is appointed the policeman and seeks to find the thief, and in the other, the "I" is not at all concerned with the "me". It is not a matter of seeking the source of thoughts based on the "me" and then wandering into the source of particular thoughts, into the realms of memory and perception. All this mental activity would belong to the "me" concept, the mind which itself is the thief trying to locate the thief. What is to be enquired into is the source of the "me" (mind) and not memory or perception which are the attributes of the mind itself. Perception or memory or any other experience, being only a modification of the mind, concerns the very "me" whose source is to be located through Self-enquiry.

All memory, all experiences disappear during deep sleep. You came from the same source in which you remained during sleep, except that whilst asleep you did not know where you remained. This is the reason Self-enquiry must take place during the waking state. *That which was present in your deep sleep, enabling you to say that you slept well or not, is Your true Self; that which was ignorant in sleep of the illusory "me".*

*Avidya* (ignorance) arises on *vidya* (knowledge) like ripples and waves arise on the surface of the ocean, and *avidya* dissolves in *vidya* just like the ripples and waves dissolve in the ocean. There is truly no difference between the waves and the water; similarly the distinction between ignorance and knowledge is notional and unreal. What exists, when ignorance and knowledge are no longer seen as two distinct entities, is Truth. The reflection of *vidya* within itself is considered *avidya* (ignorance), and when both these notions are abandoned, what remains is the Truth, phenomenally a void but noumenally the potential plenum or fullness. It is the reality in all things like the space within several pots. It causes cosmic movement and phenomenal manifestation without the slightest intention of doing so. It must because that is its nature, just like a magnet makes iron filings move, merely by its presence.

Thus all phenomenal manifestation (with all the sentient and insentient things in it) is really nothing but an appearance, an illusion. *Nothing has really been created as physical or material.* When conceptualization ceases, all notions of being and non-being disappear. It is then realized that all the supposed individuals with supposed independence and autonomy are merely empty expressions. All relationships that seemed so significant are truly non-existent and imaginary. Even when the rope is mistaken for a snake, can one be bitten by such an imagined snake though it may appear very real?

Absence of Self-knowledge is *avidya*. When Consciousness objectifies itself and regards itself as its own object of observation, there is *avidya*. When this notion of subject/object relationship gets abandoned, what remains is Reality or Truth. Individuality is nothing but the personalization of Consciousness resulting in what is known as the mind. So long as this personalizing of Consciousness remains, so long must remain the *notion* of an individual and his bondage. So long as there is a pot, there must necessarily be the notion of space within that particular pot. When the pot is broken, there is no enclosed space.

The fact of the matter is that all there is, is Consciousness, which is our true nature. As part of the totality of manifestation we are nothing but Consciousness, which is immanent in all manifestation. What has happened is that a spurious or false "me" has arisen between the universal Consciousness (which is immanent in all that is manifested) and the insentient body. The "me" imagines itself to be confined and limited to the particular body. What Self-enquiry does is to seek the source of this spurious or false "me" by focusing on it the spotlight of attention or awareness, whereupon the "me" vanishes at once because it does not have any independent existence and is merely an illusion. Whatever the religion or the *sadhana*, the basic aim has always been the elimination of this ego.

It should be evident from this that there are two selves in a man, a true Self and a false or spurious one. All that is conveyed, by whatever words that may be used, is the essential fact that by seeing the very illusoriness of the ego (the "me"), one's true identity as the universal Self or Consciousness gets firmly established. To see the Self — the universal or impersonal Consciousness — is to *be* the Self. Otherwise the "me" is not demolished and duality will continue to remain.

Self-knowledge is not meant for one whose intellect has been deadened by a firm belief in the reality of the illusory entity in the phenomenal world, and thus pursues the illusory pleasures of the senses. Such a person who has objectivized the phenomenal world in his mind, does not realize that it is the same illusory mind which also destroys the world. For such a person, there exists the notion of birth and death and rebirth.

The individual *jiva* who thinks it is born and will therefore die is nothing but the universal Consciousness which has limited itself to the individual body. It considers itself a separate entity and therefore suffers pain and misery.

Occasionally it enjoys the pleasure which has *within itself* the *source* of pain and misery. Every moment countless beings are born and countless others die. These are spontaneous acts of creation and destruction, integration and disintegration. The process is itself purely conceptual, the consequence of the thought I Am within the Consciousness at rest.

Thus when objectivity arises in Consciousness, the Consciousness becomes limited and conditioned — that is bondage. When, as a result of apperception, the objectivity is lost, Consciousness becomes free of conceptualization and thought — that is liberation from the bondage. When there is apperception, the see-er and the seen are perceived as the two interrelated ends of the natural process of see-*ing* which is What-We-Are. There is no entity in such noumenal or subjective seeing. Similarly there is no experience and nothing experienced — we are the functioning called experienc-*ing*.

For the quieting of the mind there is no means more effective than Self-enquiry. The mind may subside by other means, but it will rise again. Self-enquiry is a direct method. Other methods are practiced while retaining the ego, and therefore many doubts arise, leaving the ultimate obstacle still to be dealt with. In Self-enquiry, it is only the final question that is tackled from the very beginning.

Self-enquiry is the direct path to Self-realization. It removes the obfuscation that covers the never-realized Self. Such obfuscation is itself the creation of mind and most other methods retain the mind as the basis of the method. To ask the mind to destroy the mind is like making the thief the policeman, or putting the arsonist in charge of fire engines! The only way to make the mind cease its outward activities is to turn it inward.

By steady and continuous investigation into the nature of the mind, the mind gets transformed into that to which the "me" owes its existence. The mind must necessarily depend on something gross for its existence. Identification with the body as a separate entity is what "mind" (ego) is, as "me". It is only after the "me" arises that the "you" and "he" and the other personal pronouns arise. It is for this reason that the source of the "me" is to be sought by Self-enquiry.

The mind turned outward results in thoughts and objectivizing. Turned inward, it destroys all other thoughts. Then the "me" concept finally destroys itself "like a stick used for stirring a burning funeral pyre itself gets consumed".

All phenomenal objects are Consciousness, because Consciousness is immanent in all phenomenal objects. Therefore both passion and dispassion, craving and aversion are mere notions. Duality exists only in ignorance. The mind, the intellect, the ego-sense, the cosmic root-elements, the senses and all other phenomena can only be Consciousness. A single sound diversifies itself into echoes and re-echoes within itself. The universal Consciousness experiences multiplicity within itself, precisely as a dreamer dreams of diverse characters of diverse ages in diverse circumstances. The multiplicity manifests as the notions "me" and "mine", "not-me" and "not-mine".

Body is Consciousness, life is Consciousness, death is Consciousness too. When death-Consciousness comes to meet body-Consciousness where is the cause for sorrow? Just as water can be calm or in movement as ripples, Consciousness can also be at rest or in movement. The man with wisdom makes no distinction between sentient matter and insentient matter. What is observed as body and what is regarded as notion, the perishable and the imperishable, thoughts and feelings — all are manifestations in the infinite Consciousness.

When gold, heavily coated with earth, is not recognized as gold, it is ignorance, precisely as it is ignorance when Consciousness is not recognized as such in its multiplicity. Either way, whether Consciousness is recognized as such or not, Consciousness will remain Consciousness. Gold is gold whether it is recognized as such or not. The only apparent or notional difference is that when ignorance is dispelled, it is regarded that gold "becomes" gold and Consciousness "becomes" Consciousness!

The truth is simple: All things exist in Consciousness, all things flow from Consciousness, all things *are* Consciousness, because Consciousness is all there is.

It must be clearly understood that whilst intellectual argument may be used — and may even be necessary at the initial stage in the process of Self-enquiry — *the argument itself is not Self-enquiry.*

The argument could run as follows: The food-body (*annamaya-kosha*) and its functions are obviously not "I". The body ages and dies, but "I" can feel myself ageless and changeless. Then again, the mind (*manomayakosha*) and its functions are also not "I" because the mind is merely a conglomeration of thoughts; and all thoughts are based on the "me" concept. That which is aware of the thoughts is the individual, the "me", which functions as the operative cognizer of the existence of thoughts and their analytical sequence. Who or what is this "me" and what is its source? The "me"-cognizer as the intellect (*Vignanamayakosha*) is not an independent entity.

The "me" did not exist in deep sleep, and when it did, deep sleep changed either into a dream or the waking state. Who is this "me" in the waking state, who did not exist in deep sleep and was therefore steeped in ignorance? Such an ignorant "me" could not possibly be the subjective "I", who is always here and now, who must exist in all three states of sleeping, dreaming and waking. And the subjective "I", as the eternal substratum (the witness), is totally unaffected by the qualities of these states.

The "me" that sleeps in ignorance is the same "me" that thinks and acts in the waking state as if it were a separate entity. What is that substratum that gives the "me" the false feeling of being present as "I"? Find out its origin and *stay there*. Persistent and ceaseless questioning will dissolve the "me" into that "I".

"I" am the perceiver of this outside world which is inert, comprising trees, mountains, and rivers. "I" am not this body (which "I" can also perceive) which was created out of a drop of sperm and which lives for a very brief moment in relativity. "I" am not sound (word or expression or name) that is cognized by the inert substance that the ear is. Sound has neither form nor existence and is but a mere momentary movement (wave) in the atmosphere. Similarly "I" cannot be any of the other senses — sight, taste or touch — because they too have no identity, and *function only when consciousness is present.* "I" can therefore only be that omnipresent Self in which there is no conceptualization. "I" am the inner light. Because of Me all the senses in all the sentient beings can experience their objects. Because of Me objects acquire their apparent substantiality. Because of Me the sun has heat, the moon its cool light, the mountain its heaviness, and the water its liquidity. Because of Me manifestation appears, is perceived and is cognized.

This one Self, the inner light of Consciousness, being itself the functioning of experiencing, is the only experience, and is therefore known as the Self with "a thousand hands and a thousand eyes". And as this Self or infinite Consciousness, I am man, I am woman, I am young, I am old. I am the fragrance in flowers. I am the radiance in the light. I am the experiencing in all that is experienced. I am the very essence, the suchness in all things in the manifested universe. It is I that exist in all that exists, like sweetness in sugar, in the same way that butter exists in milk.

*I am infinity. I am intemporality.*

Ramana Maharshi has described Self-enquiry as the direct method of "diving into the Heart", seeking the source of the "me". He has made it clear that the meditation "I am not this, I am that", while being useful, is not itself the means of finding that source.

Once it is accepted that the "me" is a mere concept, all that remains is to locate the source from which the "me" concept arises. Meditating on "I am That" can only strengthen the ego. The Upanishadic text "Thou art That" is merely a piece of information that it is the Self ex-

perienced in the egoless state which is the supreme
Reality. This Reality is to be *experienced* through the
proper method; the "me" when exposed through direct
Self-enquiry vanishes and merges into its source which is
the I Am Consciousness.

Once it is realized that the Self, the I Am Consciousness,
(which is What-We-Really-Are) is not the doer but merely
a witness, it will be seen that it is not only unnecessary to
renounce our daily activities but that it is desirable to
continue our normal life. We continue with the deep
understanding that we (as phenomenal objects) are
"being lived" in the totality of the functioning of the
manifest. The supposed doership of the "me" is nothing
but an illusion. *Normal daily activities, continued without a
sense of doership are the best possible preparation for sudden
enlightenment.*

The basis of the quest for the Self is the firm conviction
that there is no dual identity of "I" and "me". So then
whenever the "me" intrudes on any activity, the awareness that the "me" is a phantom, (an illusion in the I Am
Consciousness without any substance of its own), is sufficient to drive it away. No positive action is necessary.

The deer is trapped by the sound of music and bells
and the male elephant by the proximity of the female. The
fish gets caught by the sense of taste. The moth destroys
itself by being attracted by the sight of the flame. The bee,
attracted by the perfume of the flower, gets trapped in it
and dies. Each of them perish because of only one craving,
but you have subjected yourself to all of the five tempta-
tions. How can you possibly find true happiness? The
mind weaves a web of concepts and percepts, and then
gets caught in it like the silkworm in its own cocoon. O
mind, if you keep up your flow outward towards the
sense objects, there is nothing but sorrow for you. Turn
yourself inward, and you will rest in your beingness in
peace and tranquility.

*But why, O, mind do I instruct you in this
manner? Have I not investigated into the nature
of the self and found out for myself that there is
no such thing as the mind? Have I not learned
that the mind is nothing but the illusion that has
arisen because of the false identification of Consciousness with the individual body-mind
mechanism? O mind, there is no relationship
between us: how can there be any relationship
between the infinite Consciousness that I Am and
you who are nothing but the illusory ego?*

The infinite Self cannot be squeezed into the mind just
as an elephant cannot possibly be accommodated in a little
fruit. It is Consciousness itself, by limiting itself to an
individual body-mind mechanism, that loses its universality and becomes susceptible to conceptualization and
is then known as mind.

The nature of Self-enquiry is often not clearly understood. The enquiry "who (or what) am I?" really means
an effort to find the source of the ego. This effortless effort
leads to the apperception of Truth. The intention is not to
occupy the mind with other thoughts like "I am not the
body". In fact the practice of Self-enquiry begins after the
theoretical intellectual analysis is over. Seeking the source
of the "me" does not mean replacing one thought with
another but getting rid of all thoughts. The attention is
fixed on finding the source of the "me"-concept by enquiry. Whenever a thought arises, to whom does that
thought occur? The answer must be, "to me". Then you
resume the awareness of the Self.

Self-enquiry is something quite different from the introversion of the psychologists because it is not a mental
process at all. Introversion means investigating the contents and the composition of the mind whilst the purpose
of Self-enquiry is to probe *behind the mind* to the Self. The
Self is the source from which arises the mind or the ego or
the "me"-concept. Self-enquiry, seeking the source of the

"me" who considers itself in bondage and seeks freedom therefrom, results in knowing one's true nature. This is the only Liberation.

Similarly, Self-enquiry differs fundamentally from any kind of psychiatric treatment because the latter merely aims at producing a normal integrated individual ego whereas Self-enquiry aims at *transcending* the bounds of the human individual. The common ground is that both bring up hidden thoughts and impurities buried in the depths of the mind. The point is that these *thoughts spring up spontaneously, and when thus exposed, through Self-enquiry, are promptly extinguished.*

The problem that persistently arises and bothers most seekers is: If "I" am truly the infinite Consciousness, what is this finite limitation, this illusory entity, this ego-sense, that has arisen in the infinite Consciousness? What has given rise to this "me-and-the-other" separation which is the cause of all bondage and misery?

The infinite Consciousness is the source that gives the light to the Sun and the moon, the energy that animates everything that is sentient in the universe, and provides the infinite variety in the manifestation of the universe. This infinite Consciousness, which is immanent in the three aspects of time and witnesses the functioning of the entire universe, identifies itself with each psychosomatic apparatus. It does so in order to provide the *lila*, the dream of living, so that each human being assumes for himself the subjectivity of the universal Consciousness. Thereafter, the personal consciousness assumes autonomy, independence and choice of decision and action for each human being — and thereby suffers alternating experiences in duality of pleasure and pain. When the personal consciousness realizes its universality, it sees the *lila*. It sees the enormous joke underlying the *lila*, and sees (and accepts) living for what it is — a great dream. Then all experiences in temporal duality, all the separations between the pseudo-subject and its objects (the "me-and-the-other" concept) disappear into the phenomenal void.

When delusion and confusion are gone...when the truth is realized by means of Self-enquiry...when the conceptualization ceases and the mind is at peace...when the heart suddenly opens itself to the supreme truth and is filled with the bliss of the Absolute...then there is no more restless seeking for the supposed liberation and this very world is realized as an abode of bliss. Direct experience alone is the basis of all proof. Direct experience of "What-Is" needs no illustrations as are required by mere intellectual understanding.   Illustrations have the inherent danger of being misinterpreted because they are necessarily based on temporal duality whereas "What-Is" is infinity and intemporality. In direct experiencing, there is total absence of the triad of comprehender, the thing comprehended, and the process of comprehending.

The ego-sense (with all its differentiation of me-and-the-other in space-time) arises when Consciousness becomes "aware of the savour in salt, the sweetness in sugar and the pungency in the chili". It arises when Consciousness becomes aware of the nature of a rock, a mountain, a tree, a river. It arises when the multifarious combinations of particles and molecules are seen in Consciousness as objects of the pseudo-subject instead of as mere appearances or reflections within itself. In reality there is no subject-object relation because in all such combinations Consciousness is immanent therein.

The dream of phenomenal manifestation arises in the phenomenal void because that void is not a dead nothingness but is indeed the fullness of throbbing potentiality. From the potentiality of the unknown (*Chit-akash*) arises the actuality of the known (*Mahad-akash*). When this is realized, the huge joke in the phenomenal *lila* can be enjoyed; when not understood, "life" becomes the misery of *samsara*.

There is basically no difference between the waking state and the dream except that the one seems more *stable* than the other. The contents of both states and the experiences suffered in both states are of a homogenous nature. The important and significant point is that the

dream itself is regarded as the waking state during the
process of the dream and therefore as stable as the waking
state. It is only after there is awakening from the dream
that there is realization that what we considered as the
waking state was only a dream. Similarly, it is only after
there is an "awakening" in the form of enlightenment, that
there is realization that this waking world is indeed a long
dream. The seeming permanence of the waking world is
really as much of an illusion as the dream because, in a
dream, what later (on awakening) is realized as a brief
moment is experienced by the dreamer during the dream
as a life-time or an episode lasting a long time.

The body appears very much real in a dream and its
pains and sufferings seem quite unbearable. Similarly, in
what we regard as the waking state, what seems a solid
body and its sufferings are really an illusion. They result
from a mental predisposition, a movement in Consciousness.

When there is realization that the world that appears
so real is merely a reflection of our own true nature, all
fear and delusion vanishes.

The notions of bondage and liberation are merely
modifications of the mind. As they do not have any
independent existence, there is no question of their
functioning on their own. But the point is that the very
fact of their being modifications suggests that there must
be something *here and now*, something autonomous and
independent, a substratum that is their common support
and source. Self-enquiry throws up the fact that the terms
"bondage" and "liberation" refer only to the "me"-con-
cept, and the "me" cannot exist except as a mere concept.
That which remains when the "me" disappears is the
substratum of all that is manifest, all thought and all
action. When the mind is ceaselessly directed towards the
source of "me", without any externalizing or objectivizing, then the vivid realization of this supreme Truth, this
Reality, comes about naturally and spontaneously. Then
there is a sense of wonder about the *simpleness and ordinari-
ness of the happening known as enlightenment.*

The Self that is sought through Self-enquiry is already realized. This fact must be clearly borne in mind. If the realization is something that is "caused" through the enquiry, then such realization would necessarily be time-bound like all items in duration. But surely realization is not worth seeking if it is not eternal. Therefore what is sought is not something that is to be created, but something that already exists as eternity and infinity but is hidden by obstruction. Ignorance is the obstruction. Once the ignorance (together with its interrelated counterpart "knowledge") is removed through Self-enquiry, the Truth will shine of itself. The "me-concept" is the ignorance, and as soon as its source is located, it must disappear because it has no independent existence.

*The nature of Consciousness* is such that it can simultaneously pervade the past, present, and future and experience infinite universes. It experiences the interrelated opposites, like what is sweet and what is bitter, at the same time because it is what remains when all interrelated opposites are super-imposed and cancel or negate one another. It is the tranquility and peace of the conceptual phenomenal void that is truly the potential plenum. Consciousness is, by its very nature, free from all concepts and modifications. It is ever at peace. It never loses its homogeneity, even when apparently experiencing the diversity in phenomenal objects.

When the infinite Consciousness limited itself by identification with an individual body-mind, its perception of the three modes or periods of time also started. Thus arose the concept of bondage. When the personal consciousness realizes its true nature (which was apparently veiled by conceptualization and objectivization), and abandons the concept of time as something apart from itself, it is freed from the bondage of the dualism of "me" and "not me" which is the very basis of conceptualization.

One of the difficulties expressed in regard to Self-enquiry is: Self-enquiry is supposed to be ceaseless, but how can one sit in meditation all day (even if one could physically do so) and yet carry on one's daily routine? This question is basically related to the fact that Self-enquiry is usually associated with the word "meditation", and meditation is generally thought of as something to be done at regular times, sitting cross-legged on the floor with a straight spine, eyes closed, and attention centered on the "I Am", the sense of being alive and present. But the fact is that while this is indeed the usual posture and procedure for meditation as such, a fundamental part of the process of Self-enquiry is that it not be restricted to any set hours of meditation (which could give it the feeling of a spiritual "drill") but that it be gradually extended throughout the waking hours until it becomes "the undercurrent of all thought and action".

Self-enquiry is not so much a positive process of doing some *sadhana*, but rather a negative process of letting the mind subside by seeking its source. It may begin with positive meditation at fixed times, but what happens is that as the enquiry proceeds, the undercurrent of enquiry begins to awaken spontaneously and spreads gradually to all activity *without intruding or forcing itself on the activity.*

Such ceaseless awareness of the working of the mind ultimately takes the form of witnessing whatever happens without any choosing or judging. Intruding thoughts are cut off as soon as they occur. When conceptualizing is thus nipped in the bud, undiluted attention gets centered on the activity in hand, leading to much greater efficiency, and less and less interference from the "me". Thus is achieved true meditation even during daily activity.

The tree within a seed cannot grow out of it without destroying the seed. But whereas the tree and the seed are material substance, Consciousness is formless and nameless. There is nothing other than Consciousness. Whatever may appear therein which *seems* to be of a different nature, it is Consciousness and nothing else.

The See-er is not realized so long as the self is seen as the object. One does not realize the Self-nature so long as the objective universe is perceived as such. This is because unless the duality is seen for what it is, a mere medium in which the phenomenal manifestation may be perceived and cognized (not an actuality), the subject/object division persists and the unicity of Consciousness will not be realized. If you persist in seeing the mirage as water you will never see the truth of what makes the mirage appear. But if you perceive the truth that it is the hot air that makes the mirage appear like water, the delusion of the water disappears.

It is only when the separation between the see-er and the seen is surrendered that the realization occurs that see-er and seen are merely the two necessary interrelated components of the function of seeing. And, vice versa, when realization has happened, the separation between subject and object disappears and only the functioning remains.

In *Ramana Hridayam*, Ramana Maharshi says:

> *"The Quest, Who is he to whom belong actions, separateness (from God), ignorance or separateness (from Reality), is itself the Yogas of action, of devotion, of right understanding and of mind control. That is the true state (of the Self) — the untainted and blissful experience of one's own Self — where the seeker, the 'me', being demolished, these eight have no place." (the four defects and the four remedies of Ashtanga Yoga)*

The four Yogas are based on the false identification of the seeker with the ego, which results in the attributing to the Self one or the other defect that appears in himself. The Yogi of Action pursues his yoga with the intention of neutralizing the actions of the Self as the doer of actions. The Yogi of Devotion proceeds on the basis that he is someone other than God and needs to become united with Him by devotion. The Yogi of Right Understanding intends to remove from the Self the ignorance which he thinks has enveloped the Self. The Yogi of Mind-Control considers the Self to have been separated from Reality and seeks reunion by the control of the mind.

These are wrong assumptions because the very fundamental truth is that the manifestation of the universe is itself an illusion. The individual self is merely a part of that illusory world. In other words, the Self has always been free and perfect, without the faintest taint of bondage. The seeker of the Self starts with this knowledge and through the quest, *experiences* the true Self. And in the total absence of the "me", there are neither the four defects nor the four remedies prescribed by the four Yogas.

# The Beginning Of The End Of Bondage

If it is accepted that the individual is merely an appearance in Consciousness...if it is accepted that every thought, every action, every event is a movement in Consciousness...if it is accepted that therefore a supposed individual, a mere phenomenal object, cannot be considered a cause of any event whether considered "good" or "bad"...then the question arises: to whom do the Masters and the various scriptures in every religion, address themselves? To whom do their words, their pointers, their injunctions apply? If this is merely a superficial query at the intellectual level, the discussion could go on indefinitely with philosophical arguments and counter-arguments. But if the question persists with a nagging intensity that becomes a consuming problem which refuses to go away, then it truly means the beginning of the end of the supposed bondage. Indeed, it may well mean much more than a mere beginning. It may mean the very end of bondage because, when the answer flashes with a spontaneous conviction that needs no support from any external source, the very problem of bondage gets dissolved, suddenly and instantaneously.

Since there cannot be any individual as a separate autonomous entity, the problem of bondage vanishes when it is realized that it was created by thought and therefore was merely a concept with no substance. To a conceptual problem there cannot be any valid answer except to see the problem, in perspective, as an empty thought.

Actually, what has happened is that the problem of bondage has arisen like a phantom because the premise on which it was based was not understood in its real, deep, significance. The illusoriness of the phenomenal world — and everyone and everything therein — is accepted at the intellectual level. But such acceptance of the illusoriness of the manifest world *does not include the "me" who is asking the question!* And this is what is pinpointed when the answer suddenly and spontaneously flashes into consciousness. This flash of understanding demolishes the "me" who was standing apart from the illusoriness of the rest of the world and asking the question. And with the "me" go all its problems. This flash of understanding makes a joke of the entire problem of bondage and emancipation. There is the sudden realization that all the "me's" (and "you's") are merely the objective expression of the subjective "I". This sudden realization often explodes through the human apparatus in the form of uncontrollable laughter at the primeval joke that is *maya*. It might then transform itself into such compassion (love) that a most painful need to embrace the whole world would arise.

Until this intuitive flash of understanding occurs, the logical question is: What can be done to "acquire" this flash of understanding? Again, the only answer is a counter question. Who wants to know? When Nisargadatta Maharaj asked this question to a visitor, many (including regular visitors) felt that Maharaj was evading the question. He was not. The counter question was the only answer. The one who is asking the question is the illusory individual ego. And the illusory ego, who has no real existence, is not capable of "doing" anything to "achieve" anything. The sudden flash of understanding can occur only spontaneously, "from outside". It is a sudden leap from temporality into intemporality, from finitude into infinity. It can only *happen* as a sudden movement in Consciousness, in relation to which the human being concerned is merely an instrument through which the understanding happens. Does it mean then that the human being, as an individual, has no active participation except as an apparatus? That is precisely so. The event known variously as enlightenment, awakening, freedom etc. can occur only when the time and place and the apparatus are in precise readiness to receive the happening. And also, the event, being within relative temporality, is governed entirely by the totality of functioning. And Consciousness, in which everything happens, is not governed by rules and regulations. The event is a part of the grand divine design, and the relevant apparatus, and the time and place, all form a part of the complex evolution in which every human being forms a link. Whether it is in art or science or politics or economics or spirituality, every event takes place inexorably at the precisely appropriate moment. And in that moment, every moment, the totality of functioning is in perfect balance. Everything is perfection in every moment — *here and now.*

When this realization gets absorbed in every pore of the human apparatus, the "me" (personal identification) vanishes. The apparatus becomes a vehicle of the universal Consciousness. The unnecessarily assumed burden of illusory volition by the illusory autonomous individual disappears. And all that then remains is a sense of presence without the person, which gets translated in actual life as a feeling of total freedom.

No rational or logical explanation is possible in regard to the totality of functioning and the ways of providence. The divided mind, which functions in the duality of life, is incapable of understanding the whole Mind (Consciousness) which is its own source. The shadow cannot know its own substance. An Einstein does not occur suddenly. The brain capable of receiving the theory of relativity "from outside" (as Einstein has himself said) could not possibly have been developed in one lifetime. The conditions necessary in a human apparatus to be able to produce the *Jnaneshwari* and the *Amritanubhava* at the age of sixteen could not have been produced in a Jnaneshwar in one lifetime. The conditions necessary for sudden enlightenment are produced after several lifetimes. But the series of lifetimes necessary for the final event of Self-realization do not occur to any single "soul" or entity for the simple reason that all there is at any moment is nothing but Consciousness. No sentient being can have any volition or independence of choice and action because there *is* no such thing.

The course of evolution is seen all the time in life. There are some people who are so absorbed in chasing what they consider as "happiness" that they do not have either the time or the inclination to stop and wonder if their kind of happiness is truly worth having. At the other end of the scale we find people who have fully realized what life is all about. In between the two ends, we find people at different points in the conceptual stream of evolution. Until discrimination and dispassion arise, it is no use trying to get anyone interested in spirituality — he will not be interested. Once the turning point occurs, once dispassion arises, then the personal, identified consciousness — never the illusory individual — turns inward towards its true nature. Then Self-enquiry begins. Thereafter, when conditions are suitable in a particular human apparatus (which could take many, many lives — but not of the same individual "soul" or whatever name may be given to this illusory entity), the event will occur which is known as enlightenment.

The turning point, the turning of thought back towards the Source, is itself a spontaneous happening over which the supposed individual has no control in any manner or form. It is a part of the dream-play that is called life — the totality of functioning.

Dispassion arises when the heart persistently begins to question the validity of a "happiness" based on material objects which do not have any kind of consistency or permanence. The same objects which appeared to bring happiness at one time, bring unhappiness at another. The mind then seeks other objects which too suffer from the same deficiency. Pleasure and suffering come about from subject/object relationship which itself is based on certain sentient objects coming together purely by chance. All happiness and misery, based on the desire for certain objects and on relationships with other sentient objects, seems to abide in the mind and the mental attitude. And mind itself is illusory and unreal. It disappears totally in deep sleep and under sedation.

Is there a state in which it is possible not to experience any grief? Is it possible to live in this world and still maintain peace and contentment? Is it possible to live and still keep away from the current of love and hate? What precisely is liberation, upon attaining which one is supposed not to experience sorrow and to escape from birth and death? Would it then be possible to live in relationship with others, and yet keep away from the modifications and perversities of mind? These are the relevant questions.

True dispassion is not brought about by austerity or by pilgrimages or by conscious good deeds. It comes only by directly apperceiving one's true nature. The earliest stirrings of dispassion can arise only through what might be called divine Grace. In reality, this means a condition of the psychosomatic mechanism (the supposed individual) that has gradually evolved through many "lives" . These early stirrings might arise suddenly and spontaneously, but more often they come after an apparent cause, such as some serious difficulty in life or a sudden bereavement in the family.

When dispassion persists and matures, it gradually transforms itself into the spirit of Self-enquiry, which in its turn strengthens dispassion. Indeed, *dispassion, Self-enquiry and Self-realization together form an inseparable combination.*

The individual *jiva* is nothing more substantial than the limiting of the universal Consciousness by identification with the physical form. It is a mere movement of thought, giving rise to the concept of "me" and "mine". This sense of dualism or separation not being its natural state, consciousness begins the search for Unity, which actually means consciousness as the "me" searching for itself (as Unity) but unfortunately, *as an object!* When mind perceives duality, there exists non-duality only as its counterpart. When, however, the perceiving in duality ceases, there is neither duality nor non-duality. When conceptualization ceases, and there is "at-one-ment" with Consciousness, noumenal peace prevails, whatever the phenomenal psychosomatic mechanism may be doing in whatever circumstances.

To be rid of concepts like "me-and-mine" and notions such as "I am born" and "I shall die" (which are the basis of bondage), the remedy lies in Self-enquiry, which brings about the wisdom that annihilates identification. All positive efforts are as futile as trying to see one's face in a mirror that is behind ones back. It is only direct Self-knowledge, resulting from enquiry into the movements arising in one's consciousness, which acts as the *Sadguru*, the supreme preceptor. All efforts made by a supposed entity can only lead to frustration. It is only the effortless effort (passive witnessing) along the pathless path (pure understanding without a "me" as the comprehender) which can lead to the goalless goal ("That" which has always been here and now).

The question of human effort in relation to the arising of dispassion, leading to divine Grace, which in turn leads to the "path" of liberation, has always been a puzzling one. The Masters say that without human effort nothing can be achieved. But at the same time they tell us that what is destined to happen will happen. Is there any use in prayer or effort? Should we just remain idle?

What is actually meant by those apparently contradictory statements by the Masters is that it is the feeling "I do" that is the hindrance. If you are destined to do, you will not be able to avoid it — somehow you will be forced to do. It is really not your choice whether to do or not, because the individual as such does not have the independence or autonomy to have volition.

*What constitutes bondage or hindrance to enlightenment is not effort but the sense of doership.* This is the point behind the apparent contradiction that the Masters seem to teach predestination in theory but free will in practice. This also explains the affirmation by Christ that not even a sparrow can fall without the will of God, and that the very hairs on one's head are numbered.

The Koran affirms that all power, all knowledge, all Grace, are with God, and that *"He leads aright whom He will and leads astray whom He will."* And yet both Christ and the Koran exhort men to right effort. Perhaps this puzzle would resolve itself when it is seen in the perspective of the totality of functioning proceeding to unfold the play of the Grand Design. Every event — including the happening of what is known as "enlightenment" through a particular human apparatus — must fit in with the script of this drama that life is.

In the course of spiritual evolution (which may involve many "lives" but not the same individual *jiva*) the process culminating in the phenomenon of enlightenment could be *notionally* broken up or analyzed into seven stages. First, there is the thought that material pleasure is much too transitory and unstable, and that a more stable and lasting kind of happiness should be sought. This gives rise to the process of Self-enquiry which may include a search for and guidance from one or more *gurus*. At this stage, there arises a keen sense of dispassion and non-attachment, because of which the mind becomes more sensitive, more subtle and more transparent. After these three stages, there *arises* a deeper dispassion, a *natural* turning away from sense-objects and a firmer attachment towards one's real nature, whatever it might be. This attachment towards Truth takes a firmer hold of the psyche and makes it rooted, in the fifth stage, in one's true Self. The sixth stage arises when the mind, deeply rooted in the Self, ceases conceptualizing and objectivizing. The world of appearance is seen as merely the reflection of one's own true Self. The ultimate seventh stage means continuously living in the present moment (noumenal state), without any sense of doership, like a dry leaf in the breeze. This is the transcendental stage, where everything is spontaneous, natural, unbroken.

Just as an actor portrays different roles of widely differing personalities, so also the mind creates different states of consciousness, like waking and dreaming. It is the mind which experiences what it objectivizes. Indeed, mind is nothing other than the conceptualizing, the thinking. When the mind remains firmly attached to "What-Is", thought ceases, objectivization ceases, and only Reality remains. It is not by any self-effort that this happens, but only when there is perfect understanding and deep conviction. "Understanding is all". Understanding and conviction result in apperception of "What-Is". Then, consciousness, which had erroneously identified itself with the inert body, realizes its universality and the identification is annihilated. This does not involve any study of the scriptures, any self-disciplinary practices or meditative drills. All that is needed is the spontaneous instantaneous apperception in depth of "What-Is", that the totality of the phenomenal manifestation is but the objective expression of the subjective noumenon. The individual entity is inexistent, irrelevant, and both bondage and liberation are mere concepts which disappear in thin air when apperception happens. The mind becomes healed into its wholeness and holiness.

Ignorance or mental conditioning throws up a ceaseless flow of phenomenal objects through the process of objectivizing, but only until there arises a natural yearning for Self-knowledge through dispassion. A shadow remains in front only so long as you turn your back to the Sun; ignorance disappears when you turn towards the light of Self-knowledge. The firm conviction "I am not Consciousness but an individual entity" drives the personal consciousness into bondage. The firm conviction "Everything is the absolute Consciousness and the individual entity is nothing but an illusion" liberates the personal consciousness into its natural universality.

The division into interrelated opposites of subject/object, me/not-me, negative/positive etc. is merely an illusion created by thought in the split-mind. Bondage is therefore merely the bondage of the illusion of separation. When this illusion is exposed by the powerful light of Self-knowledge, the illusion of bondage disappears. What remains is what has always been — the absolute "What-Is" here and now, without the slightest taint of the space-time concept of duration which is the basis of all conceptualization.

Mental conditioning (ignorance) is like a veil over Self-knowledge, and thereby creates the delusion of pleasure and pain. When all that exists is unicity, where is the question of any "one" doing anything? While doing any and all actions that are natural to the psychosomatic apparatus, if there is no attachment to what is being done, the action is truly non-action. On the other hand, when not doing anything, it is action if there is attachment to the non-doing. If there is realization that the entire universe is like a shadow without substance of its own, like an illusion created by a magician, how can there remain any sense of doership?

The seed of the phenomenal appearance of the universe is only a thought that has arisen in Consciousness — I Am. Such thought is nothing but a concept, a mental conditioning (ignorance) that really has only a momentary existence. It seems like a continuous flow, like that of a river, because ignorance strings these moments together horizontally like beads. This ignorance veils reality. It makes unreal things appear real and reality unreal. When you attempt to grasp it, you cannot do so because such ignorance is itself an illusion. But, like a flimsy fibre that acquires strength when knitted into a rope, the illusion of ignorance, when repeated innumerable times in memory, acquires the strength of reality.

What a horrendous thing this ignorance is. But it is really only like the second moon in diplopia. It creates an illusion in the mind. One thinks the shore is moving away when sitting in a moving boat. One thinks the train one is on is moving when actually the train is still and it is the other train that is moving away. Ignorance creates the living dream and perverts all experiences and relationships in dualism. And yet the moment there is realization of the real nature of the phenomenal manifestation — that it is really like the child of a barren woman — then ignorance is exposed and annihilated. *When the flow of water ceases, the river dries up. When dualism of ignorance ceases and conceptualization stops, there is phenomenal absence and noumenal presence.*

Enquiry into ignorance, with questions such as why ignorance should have arisen at all and similar points of curiosity, is best not done. As Nisargadatta Maharaj used to say, such enquiry is like the unnecessary scratching around a particular spot on the body which *thereby* raises an itch. Once it is clearly understood that ignorance has no existence, that it is merely an illusion that has arisen as a movement in Consciousness, any further enquiries would be like projecting the future and examining the past of the child of a barren woman!

Ignorance vanishes as soon as it is examined critically. It is because of ignorance that one mistakes the silver in the mother-of-pearl. This ignorance can last only until the mother of pearl is seen for what it is. Ignorance vanishes as soon as it is apperceived that all that exists is the universal, infinite Consciousness. All phenomenal manifestations are merely appearances in Consciousness, like a mirror-effect, and are therefore illusory. All that exists is Consciousness which can be represented by the personal subjective pronoun "I".

Ignorance not being a real entity, no relationship could possibly exist between ignorance and the Self. There can be relationship only between similar entities.

The hill is not really concerned with the cloud around it. So also "I" (universal infinite Consciousness) am totally independent of any sorrow or happiness, although it might appear that "I" am associated with it. "I" am independent of the senses. The senses naturally come into contact with their respective objects without being obliged to do so by any previous conditioning. It is only ignorance or delusion to think "I see this" or "I experience that". If this position is clearly apprehended, then actions are performed naturally and spontaneously without being tainted by past mnemonic impressions. It is such spontaneous action that is truly non-action rather than inaction which is often misconceived as non-action.

In truth, Consciousness cannot really be conditioned because it is infinite and more subtle than the subtlest atom. It is from the mind, resting in the ego-notion and the reflected Consciousness in the senses, that the illusion of the self-limitation of Consciousness arises. This illusion of self-limitation and the ego acquires a false validity by the weight of mere repetition at an incredible speed. The infinite universal Consciousness that we *are* is totally untainted by any of these illusions. The hill *is* quite independent of the clouds around it.

# The Understanding That Is Pure Joy

When a visitor once remarked that in the presence of a well-known saint he felt a tremendous sense of peace and joy, Nisargadatta Maharaj asked him if that feeling was not similar to the feeling one had when relaxing in pleasant surroundings with a cool drink, after a long stint of physical exertion. The visitor was startled by the query but recovered well enough to suggest that the feeling he had was much beyond a physical satisfaction. When Maharaj further asked him if the feeling was something similar to what one felt when listening to a soulful *bhajan* (spiritual song of *bhakta* sung very feelingly), the visitor did not know what to say. What Maharaj was pointing out was that whether the joy was physical, like the ecstasy of a completely satisfying sex act, or something psychic like listening to great music, it cannot but be transitory. It is only on the surface, like waves on the sea.

What the ultimate understanding brings about is joy deep in the heart of one's being. Such joy is pure joy. It treats alike all experiences of pleasure and misery that might appear momentarily on the surface. Such pure joy, which *is* like the ultimate understanding, is denoted by the traditional term *Sat-chit-ananda* (existence-consciousness-bliss), the very essence of the source of all manifestation.

When the ultimate understanding, the apperception, takes place, this pure joy overflows in various ways. In *Ashtavakra Gita* (Chapter 2)[1], King Janaka expresses this joy in an uninhibited manner which would be totally misunderstood if it is taken as the outpouring of a personal individual. It is rather the outpouring of joy by Consciousness after it is released from the limitation of personal identity. It must be remembered, however, that whatever happens in the totality is not subject to any rules

---

1    See the authors translation w/ commentary *A Duet Of One* (Los Angeles: Advaita Press, 1989)

and regulations. Something that is expected to happen may or may not happen. A particle may or may not behave like a particle, it may behave like a wave! When understanding takes place there may not be an irrepressible cascading of joy. Thus, when enlightenment took place, the Buddha, it is said, sat for seven days in total silence. He thought: those who are destined to understand will understand even if I do not utter a word; those who are destined not to understand will not understand even if I talk incessantly; those who are destined to understand will understand through some word or some event howsoever insignificant; those who are about to awaken from sleep will awaken even through the softest sound or even the gentlest breeze, while others may not awaken even if they are roughly shaken. It is said that the great Chinese sage Lao Tzu received sudden enlightenment when he was sitting under a tree and saw a dry leaf fall from a branch of the tree. The dry leaf became his *guru.*

The briefest teaching by Ashtavakra was enough to send his disciple King Janaka into the subjective experience of the Self, which is the basis of Janaka's spontaneous outpouring into the expression of the joy of this experience.

Says Janaka:

*I am the taintless, serene, pure Consciousness, transcending nature. How long have I been fooled, deluded, bewildered by the illusion (of maya).*

*It is I alone who illumine this body and also reveal this manifested universe. (It is only because of the light of the Consciousness that all perceptions of the senses and all modifications of the mind become our experiences). Therefore, mine is all this universe — or, verily, nothing is mine. (All is mine because I am immanent in everything; nothing, because I transcend, at the same time, all that is manifested).*

*O! Having renounced the universe together with this body, I now experience the Supreme Self through some sudden wondrous wisdom that has spontaneously been awakened.*

*As waves, foam and bubbles are not different from the water on which they are formed, so the universe which has sprung up spontaneously from the Self, is not different from it. Just as cloth, when analyzed, is found to be thread and nothing else, so this manifested universe is seen, on enquiry, to be nothing but the unmanifested Self.*

*Just as sugar made from sugar-juice is permeated through and through by that juice, so the universe that has emanated from me, is permeated within and without by the "I" that is the Self.*

*The manifestation of the universe that has appeared because of the ignorance of the Self disappears (within the Self) when there is the understanding of the Self — just as the snake appears because of the non-apprehension of the rope and disappears when there is apprehension of it.*

*Light is my very essence, I am nothing other than light. It is I alone who shine when the universe manifests itself.*

*O, the wonder of it! The universe appears in me, conceived in ignorance like the silver in the mother-of-pearl, snake in the rope, water in the sunbeam (mirage).*

*Just as the pot merges into clay, the wave into water, the ornament into gold, so also the universe that has emanated from me will ultimately merge into me.*

*O, the wonder that I Am! — who knows no decay and who survives the destruction of the entire universe from Brahma, the creator, down to the lowly blade of grass. O, the wonder that I Am*

— who, though with a body, am One who neither goes anywhere nor comes from anywhere, but ever abide pervading the universe. O, the wonder that I Am — the one with incomparable competence to hold and bear the entire universe for all time without even touching it with my body. O, the wonder that I Am — who have (at the same time) nothing or all that is conceivable in thought and speech.

The triad of the knowledge, that which is to be known, and the knower, does not in fact exist, although it appears through ignorance in the taintless Consciousness that I Am.

O, the root of all misery is the sense of duality. There is no remedy for it other than the understanding that all objects of experience are illusory and that What-I-Am is the one, non-dual, pure Consciousness that is bliss.

What-I-Am is pure Consciousness. It is through ignorance that I had imposed limitations upon myself (body, mind, ego etc.). With unceasing awareness of this fact, I do abide in the Absolute Self, purged of all mental modifications. (The deep understanding of one's true nature precludes the operation of the outer world — the senses sporting with their objects — from penetrating the sanctum of one's psyche and creating any mental disturbances).

Neither with bondage nor with liberation am I concerned. The illusion has lost its support (ignorance) and it has ceased to function. O, the universe, though emanated from me (as an illusion), does not in reality exist. A conviction has arisen that the body and the universe (the body is an infinitesimal part of the whole manifested universe) are illusory, and that What-I-Am is pure Consciousness. So now that that ignorance

has been demolished, how can any conceptualizing take place?

The body-mind apparatus, heaven and hell,
bondage and liberation, anxiety and fear are all
concepts. What have I — who am pure Consciousness — to do with any of these concepts?
O, the wonder of it! I feel no duality, and the
multitude of human beings has become like a
wilderness. Towards what then should I feel any
attachment?

I am not this body. Nor do I have a body. I Am
pure Consciousness, not a jiva, a personal entity.
This indeed was my bondage, that I desired to live
(as a separate, independent entity).

O, the wonder of it! In me, the limitless ocean
(of pure Consciousness), the winds of conceptualization produce diverse world-waves instantly. With the calming of these winds, the ship of
the conceived universe, unfortunately for the
trader-jiva, gets wrecked and sinks in the limitless
ocean that I Am. (When the mind is at rest
without any conceptualizing, the ego, his ship
together with all his collected concepts, sinks into
the pure Consciousness that every human being
really is). O, the wonder of it! In the shoreless
ocean of Consciousness that I Am, the waves of
individual selves arise according to their inherent
nature, come into contact with one another, play
their respective roles (in the lila that this life is)
for a while and then disappear.

# Essence Of The Ultimate Understanding

The essence of the ultimate understanding is the in-eluctable fact that the individual human being, *as such*, does not — can not — have any volition. He is without any independence of choice of decision and action, for the simple reason that the human being is not an autonomous entity. The human being is merely an infinitesimal part of the totality of manifestation. That the human being can see, hear etc. through his senses is merely because he has, like any other sentient being (insect or animal), been endowed with sentience. That he can think is merely because he has, in addition, been endowed with intellect. In the absence of consciousness, there is no sentience, no intellect, and as far as the human being is concerned, no manifest world.

An immediate corollary of this basic understanding is the equally undeniable fact that the desire for "liberation" from the "bondage" of this life is itself a spontaneous arousal which varies from individual to individual. One person may be intensely interested in the discovery of his true Self, while another may be only superficially inter-ested and concerned only occasionally. There will be a third type who is just not interested in the subject. His only concern is with his material gains and sensual delights. The ultimate understanding comports the con-viction that no credit or blame attaches to any of these three types because none of them had any choice in the matter. Each of the types occupies a certain position in the spiritual evolution in the totality of functioning. This position is inherent. It was ingrained and impressed at the time of conception, when the father's sperm fructified in the mother's womb.

It must be clearly understood that no amount of il-lusory volition or determination or *pourasha* can bring about any substantial change. Unless, of course, that too was part of the grand design of the totality of functioning. This must be clearly understood or the sense of doership will only strengthen the ego and make the arrival of enlightenment that much more difficult. Yet even the occurrence of this understanding is a part of the total functioning!

This question of individual volition and personal effort is extremely subtle and difficult to understand. And yet it is absolutely necessary not only to understand it intellectually but to absorb it in our very being. Difficulty arises because most Masters seem to have taught predestination in theory but free will in practice! Jesus Christ affirmed that without the will of God not even a sparrow can fall, and that the very hairs on one's head are numbered. And the Koran very definitely affirms that all knowledge and power are with God and that He leads aright whom He will and leads astray whom He will. And yet both Christ and the Koran exhort men to right effort and condemn sin. The *apparent* contradiction would easily be solved if one kept in mind the concept of spiritual evolution mentioned above. The absolute illusoriness of the individual human being — and his so-called effort (*pourasha*) — will be quickly understood by the one who is on the very brim of enlightenment, whereas someone who is much lower in the scale will more easily accept the concept of effort, determination and concentration. The one whose *beeja* (seed) is basically action-oriented will tend towards *karma* Yoga because he is what is known as the "somatotonic" type, whereas the "cerebrotonic" will at once grasp with delight the principle of non-effort and non-duality without the least danger of misunderstanding. It is undoubtedly because of this inherent and basic difference between the different types of human beings — at different locations in the conceptual evolutionary scale — that the Masters have specifically enjoined that the esoteric teaching of non-duality should not be preached "in a public place". There, there would be the distinct possibility of the teaching not only being not understood, but being misunderstood. This enjoinment of the Masters takes place, of course, as a part of the total functioning. The type of human being who relies on his personal effort at one stage may, at a later stage, come to realize that such effort as is made is truly the effort in the totality of functioning and not that of any illusory individual doer.

So long as a person considers effort as his personal effort, with the purpose of achieving something, he is rejecting the all-mightiness of the Almighty. So long as a person wants something from the Almighty, he is rejecting the fact of the "Thy will be done". True love of God means surrender to Him, wanting nothing, not even salvation.

The central point of the ultimate understanding is that at any moment — in any *kshana* — there is perfection in the totality of the functioning. Whatever imperfection is seen, is seen by the imperfect mind in duration and duality. If this is clearly apperceived, no problem can arise, no apparent discrepancy or contradiction can arise. In the absence of such apperception, what prevails is the imperfect, divided mind which cannot help raising the problems. The Masters, in their great compassion, do provide answers, relevant also in duality and duration, while repeatedly asserting the imperfection of the divided mind. It cannot help the seeker if he chooses to depend only on such answers that the Masters have given and to ignore the background against which these answers were given. It must be specifically stated that it is the seeker who will lose and not the Masters. The Masters, in their wisdom, are fully aware that the understanding of the few and the misunderstanding of the many is all in the course of the *lila* that is the totality of functioning.

The questions concerning predetermination, personal volition or choice of decision, the autonomy and independence of the human being as a separate entity, and the question of time (past and future) are so intricately involved with one another, that the very essence of the ultimate understanding is nothing other than a clear understanding, at the deepest level of one's being, of this very apparent intricacy. It is "apparent" because the problem exists only in the mind, the imperfect and divided mind.

What man wants is security for the future. He cannot really be happy even if the present moment provides him with everything that his heart desires. He must have a future he can look forward to, and his experience of the past tells him that "security" has never had anything resembling permanency. It is clear to him that even if he does achieve his goal at some time in the future, the "future" does not stop with the achievement of that particular goal. What he is chasing is actually nothing better than a will-o'-the-wisp. The real tragedy of this situation is that he cannot even enjoy that which is available to him at the present moment in a large measure. But when there is true understanding, there is acceptance of the present moment—and whatever it offers—which permits a total, uninhibited enjoyment of it. It is this fact which describes the *jnani* (one who is established in Truth) as *mahabhokta*, the supreme enjoyer.

All the items which make for "insecurity" have existed since time immemorial — poverty, disease, death, war — and all along there have been a comparatively few persons of understanding who have accepted insecurity as an intrinsic part of what we call life. They have gained acceptance by using the understanding to take a qualitative jump from the relativity of involvement to the non-relativity of witnessing whatever happens as part of "living". Actually they have not *used* the understanding so much as that they have unconsciously *become* that understanding, that apperception that subjectivity is their real nature. They have accepted "What-Is" at any moment as the objective expression of their subjective being. There is no question at all of any desire to change (through the supposed volition of the supposed individual) the "What-Is" into something else. The basis of this understanding of their true nature is the conviction that the manifested universe (including the human being) is an illusion in consciousness, the appearance of which needs the concept of "space" in which tri-dimensional objects could be presented and "time" in which they could be observed. With this conviction, the human being with his intellect and volition and *pourasha* (and all the other concepts) is seen for the joke and the puppet that he is. It

requires no effort to accept that "Thy will be done" because Thee ("I", the subjective noumenon) is all there is,
immanent in and transcendental to all manifestation.

To put it simply, the essence of understanding is the
acceptance — not the reluctant acceptance of frustration
but the acceptance of utter conviction — of the fact that
life, or living, is not a stagnant pool of water but a flowing
river. It would be unhealthy to keep stagnant water for
any length of time but you cannot keep *running* water in
a bucket. If you would have running water, you must let
it flow. The flow is the very nature of the river, and change
is the very nature of life — and it must be accepted. Peace
of mind, which is what most of humanity wants, consists
not in grasping life in order to keep it secure for us, but in
"letting go". It is rather ironic that the ultimate understanding comes not by holding on to the *concepts* of God
but by relieving ourselves and letting go of all concepts
concerning God. The ultimate understanding can come
neither by straining to hang on to the material pleasures
of the world nor by making efforts to seek and grasp the
infinite absolute. It comes by accepting the finite and
relative world of living, with all its limitations and its
interrelated opposites, as the objective expression of our
own subjective Self. The universe is the objective body of
the subjective absolute.

True understanding comports the conviction that it is
impossible in life to have the pleasure that is wanted
without the pain that is not wanted. Indeed, it is most
doubtful if it would be an acceptable state to have continuous pleasure. A continuous diet of rich food would
destroy the sensitivity and appetite for food itself and
make one utterly sick! But the crux of the problem of
experiencing alternating pleasure and pain is not really in
the actual experiencing but in aligning it with a misconceived idea of "time". While the animal is happy enough
with momentary pleasure, man needs enjoyable
memories and happy expectations in order to enjoy even
his immediate pleasure. Indeed, the memories and expectations are far more real and intense than the present

pleasure or pain, because the *habit of looking ahead or behind reduces the present pleasure and increases the present pain.* This habit gives a presence to the dead past and the uncertain future, and an absence to the here and now. The only way to break this habit is to be truly convinced that change — almost continuous and ceaseless change — is the very warp and woof of the manifestation and its functioning that we call "life". And perhaps more importantly, the changefulness and transitoriness of the manifested world is the very essence of its seductive loveliness and vivacity. As has been well put, "when we fail to see that our life *is* change, we set ourselves against ourselves and become like Ouroboros, the misguided snake, who tries to eat its own tail". The important point concerning the acceptance of change as the basis of life is that such acceptance should not be a matter of compulsion or frustration but the natural result of the clear understanding that the only way to deal with change is to dive into it and become the movement.

Life presents a problem only because the individual thinks of himself as a fixed, separate entity and tries to make sense out of life from the point of view of this separate entity. What is more, organized religion has supported him in this misconceived notion of the separation of the individual from the rest of the universe. And the exhortation to "treat thy neighbor as thyself" has served only to emphasize this separation. It sets up a goal in life *for the individual.* A reward is offered in the form of unification after death with an immortal, changeless, conceived deity (God). In other words, the individual is being bribed into making an effort to fit the flow of living into a framework of rigid norms.

Misunderstanding occurs because fixed and isolated thought-words are quite incapable of describing the movement and fluidity of life, the nature of the actual experience. Therefore, instead of realizing the nature of man to be that actual experience of beingness — the sense of being alive, or being present (I Am) — man has been conditioned to regard himself as a body, a physical volume "bounded by a skin in space, and by birth and death in time." The fact of the matter is that man is an intrinsic, though infinitesimally small, part of the manifested universe. He is a pattern in a movement of convoluted evolution which began millions of years before the isolated event called "birth" and will continue long, long after the singled out event called "death". Therefore, to separate an "individual" from the rest of the universe can be nothing more than a conceptual separation. To expect perpetuity or immortality for an individual is only to want a concept or a convention to endure eternally. The ultimate understanding must comport the firmest possible conviction that man cannot be an entity independent of and separate from the totality of manifestation. The "knowledge" of the ultimate can only be the purest awareness, without any separation, of the objective expression of the absolute subject that we call life — the What-Is here and now. The "vision of God" cannot be a concept of a merciful father figure, or even a flash of blinding light, because anything like that could only be an image or concept in consciousness. You cannot give a name to It, because naming It or defining It would be to limit the limitless.

Awareness of What-Is-Here-and-Now, free from concepts, and judgments, is not intellectual knowledge. It is the reality that is sought, but such reality *cannot be an object*. Any attempt to describe this awareness must fail because the awareness that is reality comes about not by adding words and descriptions but by removing the things which prevent its experience. Much like a sculpture, it presents itself when certain parts of the material are chipped off, not when something is added to the original slab. The wanting for perfect security is one such thing that needs hacking away before awareness can present itself. It is not merely a conflict concerning the desire for security in conditions which by their very nature cannot be fixed. More importantly, it is a matter of having separated oneself from the rest of the world, which is the basis of the desire for security. In order to find security you want to separate yourself from the rest of the world. You want the rest of the world — the others — to leave you alone. Yet you find that it is this isolation itself that makes you feel insecure. The ultimate understanding includes a clear appreciation of the fact that the pursuit of security is like the tendency to hold one's breath in time of suspected danger, the longer one does it, the more painful it becomes. And this understanding is not at the usual level of being told to "face it". "Facing it" means challenging it, fighting it, and thus you are still very much involved in it. The perfect understanding of this (or any other fact) lies in *being* that fact, without any separation between a "me" and the fact of the matter.

At the root of all desire for security is the belief that there is something within us which endures through all the changes in life. The desire for security will vanish only when this belief in a "me" gives way to the faith that there is indeed the changeless within us — I Am — the Consciousness which is our true nature. This faith is indeed the essence of the ultimate understanding. It is the awareness of our true nature — here and now. This faith symbolizes the understanding that there cannot be any permanence or security in life. There cannot be any "me" or "mine" to be protected. In this awareness, there is no entity that is aware. The awareness is pure awareness, without any "one" to be aware of the awareness.

The essence of ultimate understanding is to be aware of the present moment, delinked from the past and the future. It is to discover that at each moment there is nothing other than the experience without the experiencer. Such awareness means being alert and vitally sensitive to all actions, reactions and relations in the present moment. Intent awareness is easy enough in times of pleasure or happiness, when one can forget oneself, but separation from the experience comes about quickly in times of physical or emotional pain. And yet, it is in such times of pain that it is most essential to prevent such separation. The astonishing ability of the human organism to adapt itself to both physical and psychological pain cannot come into full operation if the pain is constantly stimulated and strengthened by the tension created by the effort to escape from it.

Pain is identified as pain only because there is a memory of pleasure. Pain gets intensified by the memory of earlier pleasure. In actual fact, the brain can record only one experience at any one moment. Instead of being fully and alertly aware of a present unpleasant experience, one tries to tackle it in terms of the dead past. In an attempt to avoid the experience one tries to adapt oneself to the unknown present by comparing it with the memory of the past. This might perhaps work in cases where you can get away. An aspirin may relieve a headache. But what about things you cannot escape, like fear? The answer is *to be aware of the fear*. To be intensely aware of the fear is to realize that you *are* the fear, and therefore escape is impossible. Indeed, if naming, defining, and comparing is avoided, every experience becomes a new experience. Then there is no conflict between the experiencer and the experience because there is no resistance.

It has been the experience of most people that when resistance and tension cease, pain becomes manageable. It is no longer a frightening experience. The pain sometimes disappears altogether. When there is no resistance to (and separation from) the pain, there is no longer a problem. Then the desire to escape merges into the pain. This is easier to understand when one remembers that a fall from a height will cause much less damage when the body is relaxed. A building generally has "give" in its construction in order to better withstand a storm or an earthquake. The mind has the inherent ability of "give" so that it can absorb shocks. But it is necessary not to burden it unnecessarily with resistance or the tension of opposition (which in effect means running away from the experience). And resistance in any form or manner ("fighting it" or running away or giving in to frustration) must continue until it is realized that the thinker and the thought, the experiencer and the experience are not separate. Realization of the inevitability of pain brings

into operation the natural "give" of the mind, thus enabling it to absorb the pain and reduce its intensity. *The
experience becomes the awareness of pain without the illusory
experiencer who was afraid of the experience.*

The key to bearing pain is in the unequivocal acceptance of it as the fresh experience of the moment in total
relaxation. When this is clearly understood, the question
of how to do it should not arise. How to relax? How to
accept whatever experience the present moment brings
with total receptivity? How to breathe? How to digest
the food? To expect answers to such questions is to miss
the point altogether. Indeed, that such questions should
arise is the clear proof that man has allowed his "brain"
to develop logic and reason — linear thinking — without
maintaining a balance with its inherent intuitive wisdom.
The result is dissatisfaction, conflict, separation within
separation, and a ceaseless vicious circle.

The essence of the ultimate understanding is contained
in an extraordinary transformation in the vision of life. In
it the usual separation between "me" and the "other" is
healed so completely that the organic unity of the world
is not a mere intellectual inference but a deep and lasting
experience. It is not just a belief but a confirmed faith.
However, one must realize that this sense of unity is *not
necessarily* demonstrable in practice. While there may not
be a desire to embrace the beasts and reptiles, there is
certainly a firm conviction that our feelings about the
creepy and the slimy creatures are feelings not outside
ourselves but "the hidden aspects of our own bodies and
brains". What is realized is that the sense of unity is not
"a sort of trance, in which all form and distinction is
abolished, as if man and the universe merged into a
luminous mist of pale mauve". There is understanding
that the wide variety and multiplicity seen in the universe
are not warring opposites but complementaries like the
various organs and parts of the body. The conditioning of
separation, caused by thought-words, is seen for what it
really is. What was an inexplicable puzzle to logic and
reason becomes a ridiculously obvious matter of What-Is.

The essence of the ultimate understanding is to see the What-Is as the manifested expression of the unmanifest reality. It is seeing with the whole mind of the present moment here-and-now, without any effort to make life mean something for the individual in terms of the future.

# The State Of Enlightenment

Every atom of existence contains countless universes. All are appearances in the infinite and universal Consciousness which pervades the entire being of the atom. So each individual *jiva* experiences within itself whatever has arisen within itself because of the pervading energy. All phenomenal manifestation is nothing but a long dream and everything in the dream appears very real so long as the dream continues.

As soon as there is realization that all phenomenal manifestation is merely an appearance in Consciousness and is, therefore, illusory (except as the infinite Consciousness itself which is the real and permanent substance), then all notions of diversity and separation at once disappear. Such realization comports the realization that "time", "space", "matter", "motion" or "action", are all but different aspects of the same infinite Consciousness. Such realization is similar to the realization that the many different kinds of food preparations spread out on the table during a feast are different only in regard to their taste, shape and size. They are all created out of the same molecular ingredients.

Illusion disappears when one experiences the truth that it is on account of Consciousness that the manifestation appears in the individual *jiva*, and that there are *jiva* within *jiva*, ad infinitum. And when illusion disappears, the craving for sensorial pleasures gradually falls off. There is a realization that just as the painting of a woman's form, however beautiful and lifelike, is not the woman, so also, sensorial pleasures, however acceptable they may seem, do not make for lasting peace and happiness.

When Consciousness became aware of its existence as the pure potential plenum, when the first thought "I Am" arose in Consciousness, the nature of the occurrence was not unlike awakening from deep sleep and becoming aware of the manifestation without (but the manifestation without is actually a mirror reflection of the Consciousness within). When thus there was awareness in Consciousness with the thought "I Am", the pure elements (*tanmatra*) arose simultaneously and spontaneously. Also, all the senses (which actually are pure void of plenum) came into being. The corresponding knowledge and experience of the five elements and the five senses brought about the identification of the universal Consciousness as the ego-sense. Enlightenment brings about the disidentification from the experiences of the senses, and thereby freedom from the psychological and illusory distress of the mind.

Enlightenment brings about a transformation of perception and attitude — a *metanoesis* — whereby for the rest of the life-span, the "individual person", having lost his individuality becomes the *mahakarta*, the *mahabhokta*, the *mahatyagi*.

As a *mahakarta* (the supreme doer of actions), he is totally free of doubt, which is inevitably based on the ego-concept. Appropriate actions get performed through him in any circumstances (whether they may be considered as right or wrong according to the current social standards). The point is that his actions are not tainted by any of the multitude of mental notions and prejudices. "He" witnesses the actions with complete indifference to the results that might follow, since he is not the doer.

As a *mahabhokta* (the supreme enjoyer), he actively enjoys all the natural and spontaneous experiences which come about without any desire or effort. Even when engaged in actions, he does not grasp or cling to what would generally be considered as "acceptable", nor does he abhor or avoid and reject anything that would generally be considered "unacceptable".

As a *mahatyagi* (the supreme renouncer), he has renounced his separate individuality as the "me" opposed to the "other" and thereby has at once renounced all other interrelated opposites including birth and death, good and evil, etc. He is thus the pure witnessing of the dream-play that this life is.

After enlightenment there is the clear apprehension that just as long as there is the potent oilseed, the oil in it must exist. So also, as long as the psychosomatic apparatus known as the body exists, so long must that apparatus act in accordance with the way it is programmed to react physically and psychically to outside stimulus. As long as the body exists, so long must the physical organs respond to stimulus and so long will also naturally exist the different moods. Any resisting or rebelling against such states or reactions would be like "attacking space or empty air with a sword".

Self-realization or enlightenment comports the apprehension that the mind is not an entity but a mere notion. All notions and concepts thereafter become irrelevant. No desires arise for wanting anything that is generally considered acceptable nor is there any question of rejecting what is generally considered as unacceptable. Whatever comes unsought is welcomed and experienced. As long as the body lasts, the organs of action are free to perform their normal function, though, of course, the mind-intellect and the senses remain in a state of equanimity and detachment.

It is for this reason that the sage Vasishtha advised Rama to engage himself in natural activity which arises spontaneously and unsought, without any personal sense of grief or guilt: "Enjoy the pleasures of the world and final liberation too."

Even where there has been liberation or enlightenment or whatever, comprehension of materiality does not change while the body is engaged in day-to-day activity. It must never be forgotten that *moksha* (enlightenment) *is also a state of the mind*. The natural function of the body continues as here-to-fore. The body responds to pain or satisfaction like any other body and may weep or laugh, but, deep down, there is neither elation nor depression, but perfect equilibrium.

From Brahma down to a blade of grass all phenomenal objects are subject to two forms of "birth". The first is as a part of the totality of manifestation. The second is through the personal identification of the infinite Consciousness. When this ignorance of personal identification gets removed by apperception, the second birth is at once negated.

Enlightenment or awakening is not a state of existence like that of a rock or a vegetable. It is a state which arises consequent on the deepest possible conviction of the unicity of What-Is and of the non-difference between What-Is and what-appears. It arises after a thorough Self-enquiry, at the end of which all mental conditioning of dualism disappears altogether. It is a state of total freedom (*Kaivalya*). All that appears and all that happens is accepted as an integral part of "What-Is" and there is not the slightest desire to change anything or become anything else.

Where the seed of *vasana* or self-limitation ("me" as separate from "not me") or mental conditioning in any form remains, that state is comparable to the temporary condition of deep sleep. It is not the perfect state. Perfection comes about only when there is the deepest possible conviction of the unreality of anything that is phenomenally perceptible. Then finally even the seed of *vasana* is destroyed. This is the transcendental state of perfection, the state of pure being, when the existence of the body is totally irrelevant.

The state of perfection means the realization that the *chit-shakti*, the energy that determines the nature and characteristics of the molecules of each object, is none other than the *atma-shakti*, the energy of the universal Consciousness, which lies dormant when Consciousness is in a state of rest and erupts with the first thought "I Am".

Conversely, just as the very first thought disturbs sleep and ends it, the first awakening of inner intelligence — the very first stirring of the Self-enquiry: what is this "I" without this destructible body? — gives ignorance its death-blow. When the light of enquiry is turned on ignorance, ignorance vanishes. Can darkness remain when light is turned on to it? The light of Self-enquiry dispels the darkness of ignorance (*avidya*) which is only the belief that something other than Brahman can exist as reality.

When false perception has come to an end by the elimination of subject/object relationship, the mind is demolished and is totally ineffective, like dry leaves after they are burnt. Where apperception of the Truth has taken place, and both the "What-Is" and "what-appears" have been correctly understood in their mutual relationship of transcendence and immanence, the state of mind is known as *Satva*. Then, indeed, that state of mind could hardly be called "mind". It could be rightly described only as *Satva*. Such awakened "entities" may be engaged in their respective occupations and carry on their normal activities as if they are interested, but truly they are always in perfect equilibrium. They take life playfully accepting events as they come along. Dualistic concepts cannot arise in such people. The very seed of ignorance has been burnt beyond recovery, and they are constantly aware of the truth that they are the infinite and universal Consciousness within which innumerable universes appear and disappear like waves and ripples on the ocean water.

All apparent differences are nothing but the Self-experiencing of the Infinite. Experiencing is not different from Consciousness; the ego-sense is not different from experiencing; the *jiva* (the individual) is not different from the ego-sense; and the mind is not different or separable from the *jiva*. Are the waves separable from the ocean? The awakened being, though he appears as if he is living like any other person, really "does" nothing because he seeks nothing.

The pot may be pulverized but is the space therein destroyed? The body may be dead and buried or cremated, but is Consciousness within also thereby destroyed? When there is apperception, can the mind with its notions of happiness and unhappiness survive? *There is neither the craving for pleasure nor the desire to get rid of it.* With the wisdom of apperception comes true dispassion and there is genuine renunciation through the surrender of the conceptual "me-entity".

With the annihilation of the "me-entity" comes peace and tranquility. There is no room for confusion or doubt or delusion. Concepts of heaven and hell, birth, death and rebirth, all get annihilated along with the "me-entity". What is more, even the delusion of liberation disappears together with that of bondage because both are based on the "me" concept. And then it seems a miracle, not that the mind should be freed from the veil of ignorance, but that the mind should have been clouded and tainted by thought, percepts, concepts, desires and cravings in the first place.

With the apperception comes the conviction — or with the conviction comes the apperception — that the distinction between the universal Consciousness and the personal consciousness was only notional. It was like the distinction between the wave and the water in the wave, or between the word and that to which it refers.

A breeze flowing through certain flowers passes on their fragrance, so also Consciousness creates bodies appropriate to the notions with which it entertains and identifies itself. Through these bodies, which it energizes, it then experiences the consequences of those notions.

Enlightenment happens only when Consciousness divests itself of notions and concepts by ceasing to conceptualize. It happens only when the mind is not swayed by the pairs of interrelated opposites and when objects are not seen as though by a pseudo-subject. There is truly no transformation as such, only a demolishing of the conceptual bars of the prison of limitation, which leaves Consciousness in its unidentified, infinite universality. When the mind is cleansed of all conceptualization, it is restored to its natural wholeness. It functions in its natural smooth flow without any confusion or doubt. Waves may appear and disappear on the surface of the ocean, worlds may arise and vanish on the surface of Consciousness, but while the ignorant are swayed by the appearances, the *jnanis* are always aware of the calm equanimity of the sub-stratum beneath.

The moment enlightenment takes place, the person sees the truth that he is the infinite Consciousness which contains within itself everything that happens everywhere at all times. He is infinity and intemporality. He sees that pleasure and pain are experienced in the body through the operation of time and because of particular circumstances with which he (as the universal Consciousness) is not directly concerned. The ignorant regard the body as the source of suffering, but to the enlightened, the body is the source of infinite delight and joy. And being unattached to it, he is not sorry to part from the body when its span ends since he had always regarded it merely as an instrument.

*There is no universe independent of Consciousness* in which arise the fantasies of a moment or an epoch (both of which are assumed to be on a real time-scale, just as objects seen in dream appear to be real *at that time*). A whole epoch can be conceptualized in the mind, just as a whole city can be reflected even in a small mirror. How then can we assert the reality of either duality or non-duality? The fact is that *Consciousness itself is both the moment and the epoch, the near and the far*. It is the interrelated opposites which, on superimposition, cancel each other into a phenomenal void that is really the noumenal plenum of total potentiality.

The gold within is not perceived so long as what is seen is the bracelet. The gold is perceived only when the bracelet is seen as a mere shape that is easily changeable. When the misconception of the universe as being real is discarded, what remains is Consciousness. Total objective absence is total subjective presence.

When the Self has been attained, nothing has been attained! The inner and the outer, the Self and the non-self are mere words without any significance or substance, used only for the benefit of the ignorant. When the external object is seen as such, the pseudo-subject is created. Actually all there is is the see-*ing*, there is neither the see-*er* nor the object seen. When the mnemonic impressions have ceased, the pseudo-subject no longer exists and without the supposed subject, the object cannot exist either. The noumenon, as the subject, exists because of the object, and the phenomenal object is but a reflection of the subject. Duality can exist only as the interrelated opposite of non-duality. *Where is the question of union or unity if all there is is unicity?* The goldness of the gold is always there. The question of duality arises only when there is a name and form as a bracelet. That which is beyond all interrelated opposites is the Absolute, the Brahman. When there is apperception of this truth, all duality and non-duality disappear. What remains is not expressible in words. Such apperception happens only through Self-enquiry. As long as words are used to denote a truth, duality in the form of the interrelated opposites is inevitable. Though words are necessary to direct the attention of the ignorant to the truth, words are *not* the truth.

Apperception of the truth leads to the direct experience of non-duality. The ego-sense and the previous conditioning drop off. There is no compulsive feeling "me" and "mine" nor the sense of acceptable and non-acceptable. The body-mind apparatus functions "as if in deep sleep."

The desires that arise in such a state of liberation are in the course of the natural functions and are devoid of any craving for external objects. Such basic desires that existed even prior to contact with sense objects continue to exist. They are natural, spontaneous, not based on thought, and therefore free of the impurity of dualism. Truth is non-dual, but all action necessarily involves duality because all functioning can only take place in apparent duality. Indeed, apperception comports the understanding that any difference between duality and non-duality is purely conceptual. Duality and non-duality are a pair of interrelated opposites, like innumerable other such polarities without which manifestation could not take place. When all concepts cease, when conceptualization itself ceases, what remains is the unicity of the Absolute.

When apperception occurs, all events assume a sense of unreality because they are nothing but mere movements in Consciousness. And Consciousness is our true nature.

# The Final Truth

The final truth is that ultimate understanding in which there is no comprehender to comprehend the final truth.

If you were asked who you were, your answer would obviously be to give your full name and such bio-data as may be expected in the circumstances. Your answer to the question "Who are you?" would then be accurate and precisely what was expected. But it would not be the truth!

The truth is that you are not what you appear to be. Whatever your friends and foes may think of you and whatever you yourself may think from the viewpoint of your physical, mental and moral attributes — it will all be images liable to frequent changes. So then what precisely are you?

Science takes a closer, deeper look at you and tells you that deep down you are "nothing". The scientist discovers that the human being is actually a collection of limbs and organs that are themselves collections of minute living creatures named by science as cells. Cells, in their turn, are themselves collections of particles. This process carried to its extreme conclusion leads to the undeniable fact that in the end, there is no you at all. You who appeared to others as an individual entity with a form and substance, and a certain mental image, just do not exist. You are, *as yourself*, just nothing. In other words, whatever you may think you are, whatever others may think you are, actually you are "nothing". You are simply the vibration of energy in a particular pattern, a dance of invisible particles and waves. This is the magnified view of you which the sub atomic physicist takes.

Science can also go to the other end and take a long-range view of you against the background of your surroundings, that is to say, your existence in relation to the world. The sub-atomic physicist knows that as an individual body you are nothing. But what are you, as an appearance, when the world is taken as a whole? What is the astrophysicists view of you?

(That *was* the Final Truth)

What are you when the world is considered as a whole of which you form a minuscule but essential part? What will "you" appear to be when viewed from longer and longer distances? What happens then is that the "you" first merges into the room you stand in, then to the house, then to the city and so on, until you are the world, until you are the universe from the viewpoint of infinitude. The whole point is that "you" just do not exist as an individual entity. You are either "nothing" or "everything". Either way, the startling conclusion is inescapable: I am not what I appear to be; I am not what I thought I was. Acceptance of this conclusion, even at the intellectual level to start with, will lead to a lasting faith if you take the time, as often as possible, to sit for a while quietly. Let your body relax, let your mind cease its usual chatter, and turn your mental gaze inward. If you do this, there may occur realization (if there is Grace, if this fits in with the divine plan of the functioning of the totality), realization that the nothingness that you are is not the emptiness of the void but the fullness of the plenum, realization that "your" body is but an instrument (with eyes, ears and brains) which Consciousness uses in its functioning.

Such a realization of one's phenomenal absence as a separate entity is tantamount to the realization of our subjective noumenal presence with the whole universe as our objective body. And such realization, say the Masters (the Sufi — the Advaitan — the Taoist), is Enlightenment: *I exist as phenomenal absence, but the phenomenal appearance is my Self.*

Such realization translates itself in actual life as the actionless action of pure witnessing. Pure witnessing is of a dimension radically different from space-time, and is clearly to be distinguished from a mere movement in mind because:

> (a) there is in witnessing no "witnesser" as an individual entity,

(b) there is no judging of what is witnessed as being "good" or "bad", and therefore,

(c) there is no desire to change "What-Is" in any shape or form.

In other words, such realization leads to an effortless gliding through life with a willing acceptance of whatever life might bring.

The final truth, therefore, is that the subjective "I" is all that exists. It witnesses the phenomenal manifestation (including all the "me"s) and its functioning, and is not aware of Itself when there is no phenomenal manifestation to witness.

# Also By Ramesh S. Balsekar

## A Duet of One
Here Ramesh uses the *Ashtavakra Gita* as a vehicle for an illuminating look at the nature of duality and dualism
Softcover — 224 Pages  $16.00

## Experiencing The Teaching
In this book many facets of Advaita (non-duality) are examined and illuminated through a series of 24 dialogues. Ramesh's ability to cut through to the simple heart of complex ideas is a joy to experience.
Softcover — 142 Pages $11.95

## The Final Truth
A comprehensive and powerful look at Advaita from the arising of I AM to the final dissolution into identification as Pure Consciousness.
Softcover — 240 Pages  $16.00

## Your Head In The Tiger's Mouth
A superb overview of the Teaching. Transcribed portions of talks Ramesh gave in his home in Bombay during 1996 and 1997.
Softcover — 472 Pages  $24.00

## A Net Of Jewels
A handsome gift volume of jewels of Advaita, selections from Ramesh's writings presented in the format of twice daily meditations.
Hardcover — 384 Pages  $25.00

## Consciousness Speaks
Ramesh's most accessible and easy to understand book. Recommended both for the newcomer to Advaita and the more knowledgeable student of the subject.
Softcover — 392 Pages  $19.00

## Ripples
A brief and concise introduction to Ramesh's Teaching. Perfect to give to friends.
Softcover — 44 Pages  $6.00

# If unavailable at your bookstore, these titles may be ordered directly from Advaita Press.

Send check or money order or Visa/Mastercard number (include expiration date) for the indicated amount plus shipping as noted below to:

Advaita Press
P.O. Box 3479 CS3
Redondo Beach, CA 90277
USA

**Shipping & Handling:**
**In U.S.** — — — *Surface mail*: First book $3.00. Add 50¢ for each additional book.
*Airmail*: First book $5.50. Add 50¢ for each additional book.
**Outside U.S.** — *Airmail*: $10.00 per book. *Surface mail*: $3 per book  Payment in U.S. dollars via check or money order payable on a U.S. bank. No Eurochecks please.

# More Books About Advaita

## NO WAY -
### for the Spiritually Advanced
by Ram Tzu

Blending paradox, wit, satire and profound insight Ram Tzu creates a view of spirituality that is truly unique.

*"Ram Tzu is accessible from several levels of misunderstanding."* ~ Ram Tzu
Softcover — 112 Pages $13.00

## Consciousness and the Absolute
edited by Jean Dunn

The final translated talks of Sri Nisargadatta Maharaj, recorded just before his death in 1981. Includes four b/w photos.
Softcover — 118 Pages $12.00

## I Am That - Conversations with Sri Nisargadatta Maharaj
A compilation by Maurice Frydman of Maharaj's conversations with seekers who came to him from around the world. This is the latest high quality American edition.
Softcover — 576 Pages $24.95

## Seeds of Consciousness
edited by Jean Dunn

More translations of conversations with Nisargadatta Maharaj. This is a NEW EDITION of a once out of print title.
Softcover " 216 Pages $14.00

## Prior To Consciousness
edited by Jean Dunn

Further insights into the teachings of Sri Nisargadatta Maharaj via translated accounts of his talks. NEW EDITION includes 5 new photographs.
Softcover —159 Pages $14.00

# If unavailable at your bookstore, these titles may be ordered directly from Advaita Press.

— See previous page for ordering information —

*Audio and Video Tapes Are Also Available*

*— Write Us For a Free Catalogue—*

*Or visit us on the Internet at: www.advaita.org*